MECHANICS·
MERCANTILE
LIBRARY.

Arthur F. Mathews '06

Water

The Final Resource

How the politics of water will impact on the world

by William Houston & Robin Griffiths

HARRIMAN HOUSE LTD

3A Penns Road
Petersfield
Hampshire
GU32 2EW
GREAT BRITAIN

Tel: +44 (0)1730 233870
Fax: +44 (0)1730 233880
Email: enquiries@harriman-house.com
Website: www.harriman-house.com

First published in Great Britain in 2008 by Harriman House.

Copyright: © Harriman House Ltd

The right of William Houston & Robin Griffiths to be identified as the authors has been
asserted in accordance with the Copyright, Design and Patents Act 1988.

978-1-905641-66-6

British Library Cataloguing in Publication Data
A CIP catalogue record for this book can be obtained from the British Library.

Printed and bound by CPI Antony Rowe.

To Averil

Contents

About the Authors

William Houston joined the Royal Navy at the end of the Second World War and specialised in weapons. After leaving the Service, he qualified as a Chartered Engineer and in administration before embarking on a career as a 'company doctor' – advising a large range of industrial and commercial concerns. There followed a period acting as industrial advisor to a City merchant bank.

His first book, *Avoiding Adversity,* was published in 1989 and warned businessmen of the coming recession, shortly to be followed by *Meltdown* and *Riding the Business Cycle,* which warned of the growing disruption that would take place early in the next century.

Robin Griffiths joined Phillips & Drew in 1966, having taken a degree in Economics at Nottingham University. He went on to be a partner at WI Carr, the first British stock broker to have offices in Hong Kong and Tokyo. Part of this firm was acquired by Grieveson Grant, with whom Robin enjoyed a stay in Japan. In 1986 Robin joined James Capel, which was already owned by HSBC. He stayed there until normal retirement age, and during that period travelled all over the world to meet their extended client base. For the last six years of that employment Robin was resident in New York.

Having left HSBC Investment Bank in 2002, Robin then joined Rathbones as Head of Global Investment Strategy, where he stayed until 2008. He is currently the Technical Strategist for Cazenove Capital and manages the Worldwide Absolute Return hedge fund.

Robin has been a regular on *CNN, CNBC, Reuters* and *Bloomberg TV*. He is a committee member and former chairman of the international Federation of Technical Analysts, and former chairman, now fellow, of the British Society of Technical Analysts. A keen sailor, Robin has crossed the Atlantic five times, setting a new British record in 1984 with Sir Robin Knox-Johnston.

Acknowledgements

It would not have been possible to write this book without a number of references, and we have done our best to acknowledge these in the text and in the References section at the end of each chapter. We do apologise if any of these have been left out and any errors are entirely our own.

We have also had help and encouragement from a number of people, for which we are most grateful. It is not possible to identify them all, but we have received particular help and guidance from Larry Acker, Michael Boyce, Mehdi Chaouky, Dick Fox, Ian Fridlington, Evelyn Garriss, Ian Gordon, Stephen Hill, Graham Hillier, Lacy Hunt, John Lawton, Stephen Lewis, Jacob Rees-Mogg, Ian Notley, Marc Nuttle, Deborah Owen, Christeen Skinner, Peter Warburton, Stephan Wrobel and Alan Robertson.

We would also like to thank the team at Harriman for publishing the book at a time when water is becoming such an important global issue. In particular, we would like to thank our editor Stephen Eckett for his many useful insights and suggestions. Our thanks also are to Averil Houston for taking time out of her busy life to read the proofs and for making many beneficial changes.

William Houston
Robin Griffiths

April 2008

Introduction

The rain is plenteous but, by God's decree, only a third is meant for you and me;

Two-thirds are taken by the growing things, or vanish Heavenwards on vapour's wings.

Nor does it mathematically fall with social equity on one and all.

The population's habit is to grow in every region where the water's low;

Nature is blamed for failings that are Man's, and well-run rivers have to change their plans.

'Water' by Sir Alan Herbert

We cannot do without water; without it our kidneys fail and we die. This incredible molecule was originally formed over four billion years ago as the earth started to cool, and the vapour condensed to create the great oceans where nearly 98% of all water resides; unlike many other substances, the amount of water has remained fixed since the earth formed.

We only receive it courtesy of the sun, which sucks vapour from the seas and with the assistance from the world's rotation helps move it towards the poles, bringing heat with it. As it falls over land, heat is given out, but at the most only around 10% of the water remains after run-offs before the evaporation cycle begins again.

We are also indebted to the sun for directing *where* the rain falls. This is decided by the relative position of the warm and damp air coming from the equator and the cool air from the poles. We are also blessed by the 23½ degree inclination of the earth to the sun. As the sun moves north and south relative to the earth this creates the seasons, enabling wheat to be grown as far north as Canada and as far south as Patagonia.

All this works well until the ocean oscillations, which have their own rhythms, change so that areas expecting rain suffer drought, and those previously expecting drought often experience flooding. This is exactly what is currently happening and the purpose of this book is to explain why this happens and how our lives could be turned upside down because of it.

We start by explaining that only in the last hundred years have we measured ocean temperatures and learned that the Atlantic becomes warmer and cooler over an oscillation of around seventy years. Until 1995 it was relatively cool, pushing the rain belts further south and bringing rain to countries around the Mediterranean, the Middle East and much of the western and eastern parts of the United States. Then the Gulf Stream became stronger, bringing the rain belts further north and denying much of the rain to where it had previously fallen. A similar oscillation in the Pacific may prove more serious.

Up to the year 2000, the Pacific was unusually warm and was punctuated regularly by an effect called an El Nino that moved the rain belts east, providing excellent moisture for the west coast of the Americas. Now the oscillation has changed to a cooler La Nina, which makes the great ocean unusually cool and shifts the rain belts west and south. Now, around a fifth of the world's population will receive much less rain than expected. This is partly explained by a secular solar cycle of some five hundred years that is expanding the tropics, moving the deserts further towards the poles.

We might also experience increased volcanic activity, such as the eruptions that wrecked many holidays during 2007 by altering the weather patterns. A large eruption has the force of many fusion bombs and ejects millions of tons of dust and sulphurous acid into the stratosphere, these spread towards the poles shielding the sun. The debris forces the cool polar air and rain belts towards the equator. After Krakatoa erupted in 1883, the earth's temperature fell by around 2 degrees Fahrenheit – equivalent to all of us in the Northern Hemisphere feeling we were living 600 miles further north. It also critically disturbed vital crop growing patterns.

Volcanoes occur at the edges of the plates that cover the earth and are continually shifting. These plates are helped by the movement of our satellite, which exerts maximum pressure twice a month at the time of the full and new moon to generate high tides; even higher water pressures are caused every 17.9 years in a lunar precession cycle that is next due in 2010. More immediately there is the possibility of a major climatic upset caused when, during 2008, the moon (at its perigee) is the closest to the earth it's been for 300 years. These, plus the possibility that the sun's output may be exceptionally low for the next few years, are likely to result in the more dangerous complications described later in the book – and are made worse by the wasting of water in many countries obliged to irrigate their fields.

Chapter 2 explains how water circulates, is used and misused. This is very important because so much precious water is allowed to run to waste – particularly in hot countries where evaporation is the highest. We explain how water is re-cycled, is generated from salt water, and how water can be saved from the 40% of arable land that is irrigated. As with a large eruption, the climatic shifts described earlier also affect our ability to grow food.

There are approximately 1.5 billion hectares of arable land in the world, of which around one third is being progressively destroyed by topsoil thinning, over-tilling, salt deposits, excessive logging, or just running out of water such as increasing desertification. Already, main wheat-growing areas that used to feed millions, such as the Yellow River delta, are becoming unfit for use through pollution and upstream abstraction, and the climatic shifts are reducing previously productive areas in the US and Australia. This is a situation that calls for urgent action otherwise it will cause distress to many lives.

Work done in the last century explains how the climatic shifts can also affect our lives and our outlook. Professor Raymond Wheeler of Kansas University analysed tens of thousands of historical incidents where the climate had a direct impact on people's actions. Relating the alternatives of warm/cool and wet/dry he derived a hundred-year cycle and explained how people were likely to react to each phase. Bringing this up to date, the chapter explains how different countries could react to the climatic shifts and, in particular, how millions of refugees may be forced to move.

Throughout history there have been regular mass movements of people, often taking with them diseases for which their hosts had no immunity. Most of these migrations have been climatically driven, but there have also been political expulsions for reasons of religion and envy; those expelled have invariably enriched their host country. We are now entering a period where the climatic shifts could move millions of people, causing untold disruption. That, together with a lack of water, could trigger major conflicts.

The first, and most obvious, is in the Middle East, where the ocean oscillations are likely to render areas exceptionally dry, where before there had been enough rain for a rapid rise in population. Chapter 6 explains how the control of the great rivers and improving agriculture – particularly irrigation – could create a natural conduit for peace negotiations. Conflicts in the Far East could become even more dangerous.

China is one of the countries with the lowest water availability per head of population in the world. However, despite this, rapid industrialisation and lack of water treatment have polluted the great rivers, and the ocean oscillations, together with increasing desertification, are causing those in the north to dry up. While most eyes are looking for a potential conflict over Taiwan, it will probably be over water that China, Pakistan and North Korea will be forced to address their own deficits. But some help could be at hand from technology.

There are already many desalination plants using fossil fuels but the rapid rise in evaporating fresh water from salt water may come from advances in solar energy that will make the process economic even in temperate latitudes; cold fusion – harnessing the power of the sun safely to provide heat – could further reduce our need for fossil fuels. There remains the opportunity for using hydrogen in fuel cells that will need even less energy from oil. The final chapter directs the reader towards present and future investment opportunities.

If problems over water were not enough, we recognise from our work leading to *Future Storm*[1] that difficulties over water may be paralleled by grave instability in the global credit system and from aggressive religious terrorism. This will impose on those managing affairs a most unwelcome set of conditions that will utterly transcend beliefs and practices established over decades, even centuries. We put forward alternative scenarios showing how these may evolve, and in our next book set out an approach towards their solution.

William Houston

Robin Griffiths

---

[1] *Future Storm,* by the authors (Harriman House, 2006).

1

The Cycles of Climate and Water

Summary

Over the centuries climate has played an important part in political, military, social and economic life. In the last two hundred years it has stopped two invasions of Russia, it was in part responsible for the violence of the French revolution, the Allies' success at Waterloo, and led directly to the repeal of the Corn Laws in 1842 during what was known as the 'Hungry Forties'. It continues to play an increasing part in our lives.

Whether or not there is adequate water to sustain life is the direct result of weather patterns that are primarily affected by the sun but also by periodic oscillations in the great oceans and by volcanic action. The latter part of the twentieth century saw a particularly benign pattern of climatic shifts that are likely to become sinister in the early decades of the twenty-first century.

Should these oscillations be accompanied by the major volcanic eruptions likely through 2008, they could totally overturn most of the assumptions that governments, business and individuals have in planning for the future. It is the wise general, politician or businessman that makes the climate their friend.

Introduction

The sun is the main driving force of our climate, controlling the circulation of air and the power of the oceans, but there are other determinants such as the action of the moon on the tides and the likely association with seismic action. The tsunami on December 26th 2004 and the later Pakistan earthquake, were caused by movements deep within the earth and had a profound impact on people's lives. For example, on April 9th 1815, Tambora ejected 35 cubic miles of dust and several million tons of gas high into the stratosphere, where it spread around the Northern Hemisphere. By 1816 the earth's temperature had cooled by several degrees, causing widespread crop failure and, riots, and many died of starvation and disease. It was dubbed "the year without a summer".

By early 2008 it was apparent that five important forces were at work:

1. The sun's output is the highest for around ten thousand years, which is probably the true cause of observed global warming.

2. The 11.2 year sunspot cycle, which reached a low point in 2006, may now be recovering.

3. There are oscillations in the North Atlantic and the Pacific that were benign until around the turn of the century, and are now likely to be adverse until around the third decade.

4. The closest lunar perigee for around 300 years will occur in 2008. The moon has a disproportionate gravitational impact on the earth and an unusual closeness could trigger seismic and volcanic action.

5. There is concern among some scientific, and many political, circles that mankind's carbon emissions are responsible for much of the observed rising temperatures around the earth. However, the overwhelming greenhouse gas is water vapour, that constitutes 94.5% of its total. Taking this into account, mankind's contribution to the rise in carbon dioxide – itself a minority gas that includes methane and nitrous oxide – is a pitifully small 0.3%. Of course all efforts to reduce pollution and the re-use of essential elements are important, but it seems unbelievable that politicians in the Western world should feel obliged to turn their countries upside down for such a slender reduction of global temperatures.

The influence of the sun

The conventional view of the sun's output is a cycle of around eleven years when, what are known as sunspots, go through a cycle of waxing and waning to cause temperature differences on earth, usually a fraction of a degree. Taken together with other factors, these differences are significant. The cycle peaked in 2000 and, having reached a minimum in 2006, is now scheduled to attain the next high in 2011-12. Yet something unusual is happening: the sunspots are remaining very low.

This happened four times in the last millennium. There are records of sunspots going back over many centuries that show periods of very low solar output occurring every 180 years or so. The first, called the *Wolf Minimum*, early in the fourteenth century, caused terrible famines in 1317-8 that reduced people's immune deficiency for the following Black Death. The next was the *Sporer Minimum* around 1500 that caused four famines in England in the years after. The most serious was the *Maunder Minimum* (also known as the Little Ice Age) in the seventeenth century (which is described in more detail in *Riding the Business Cycle* – see References). Finally, there was the *Dalton Minimum* (or Sabine Minimum) that initiated a very cool period early in the nineteenth century that almost certainly was responsible for Napoleon's defeat in 1812.

Professor Rhodes Fairbridge of Columbia University suggests that these minima are caused by out-of-balance movements of the great planets Jupiter and Saturn that distort the sun's output. They also cause extreme high tides on earth that cause the volcanic action described in more detail in the crustal cycle later in the chapter. The last planetary cycle top was on April 20th 1990, but at least 50% of the time the sunspot minima have been displaced by twenty to fifty years. Some scientists are not in agreement on the cause of the intensity of the sunspot cycle; nor are they in accord of work done by Sami K. Solanki of Germany's Max Planck Institute, who suggests the observed warming of the earth is due to the sun's highest activity for the last 8,000 years.

Work done in 2006 by the Sierra Environmental Studies Foundation of California and other centres – see References – suggests that during the Maunder Minimum sunspots remained very low for some five eleven-year cycles and those for the Dalton (from 1798 to 1826) were low for two rhythms; even so, they reduced the global temperature on average by up to 3 degrees Fahrenheit – equivalent to living some 900 miles further away from the equator. Opinions are divided whether the next cycle (Cycle 24) will follow the pattern of the Dalton but are at one in believing the next (Cycle 25 destined to bottom in the early 2020s) will be another minimum. Observations will show which is correct.

Long-term oscillations of the oceans

Of more immediate relevance is a paper produced by the University of Arizona that describes two oscillations:

- There is one in the Pacific that has a cycle length of around fifty years called the *Pacific Decadal Oscillation* (PDO).
- That in the Atlantic has a duration nearer seventy years and is called the *Atlantic Miticadal Oscillation* (AMO).

The records go back to 1895, with the following chart showing the positive and negative passage of the two oscillations.

Diagram 1. The periodic oscillation of the great oceans

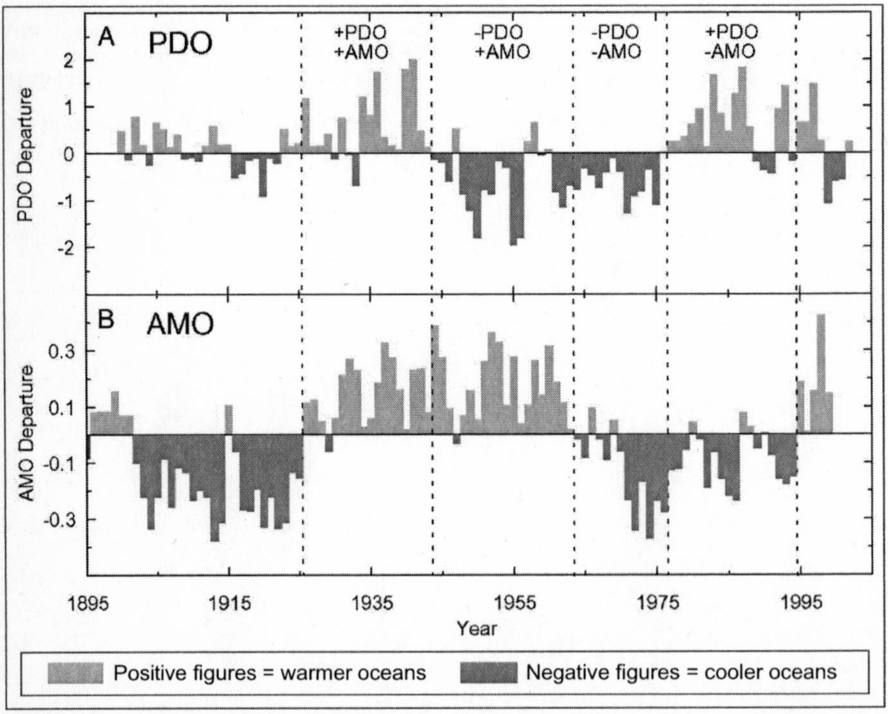

Source: University of Arizona

Pacific Oscillation

The Pacific Oscillation (PDO) has a see-saw pattern of temperature variations that are less definitive than those of the Atlantic – probably because of the occasional warming El Nino that occurs every seven or so years. In its positive phase, the rain belts move east to warm the East Pacific, so bringing rain to the West Coast of the Americas and dry seasons to South East Asia. It has been during this phase that Northern China, Central Asia and parts of the Middle East have had adequate rainfall.

In the negative phase, the rain belts move south and west to South East Asia, while the west of the Americas becomes cooler and dryer. As the rain belts move south, the areas of northern China and points west become dryer. This latter phase started in around 2000. Combined with a warmer Atlantic, this is the most dangerous condition for many areas expecting adequate rainfall.

Atlantic Oscillation

The Atlantic Oscillation (AMO) combines the North Atlantic Oscillation (NAO) with other lesser phenomena. Instead of there being differential cooling east and west, an active Gulf Stream makes the whole of the North Atlantic either cooler or warmer than normal. A warmer ocean is known as a positive AMO; a cooler phase, negative.

Normally, the greatest impact of a positive AMO is to move the storm tracks further north, creating drought conditions in south-eastern parts of the USA, and the warmer waters generate more hurricanes. To the east, the Mediterranean (including portions of the Middle East) becomes dryer, and southern Europe is more likely to experience heatwaves. The summer of 2003 was typical of this condition. The summer of 2007, while bringing heatwaves to central Europe, was modified by volcanic action in the Kamchatka Peninsula, causing unusually heavy flooding in north-west Europe.

With a negative AMO, the rain belts move further south, providing good growing conditions in eastern and central USA, southern Europe and the Middle East.

These oscillations provide four alternative combinations

There are clearly four combinations of the PDO and AMO over the fifty or seventy years of the periodicity, but other influences are at work that sometimes makes their effect variable. These are shown on the diagrams of the US below.

Diagram 2. The impact of the Atlantic and Pacific Oscillations on US climate

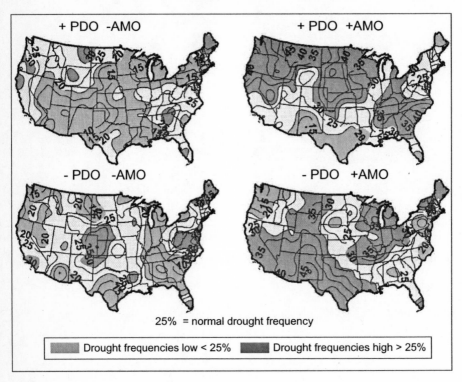

+ PDO -AMO   + PDO +AMO

- PDO -AMO   - PDO +AMO

25% = normal drought frequency

Drought frequencies low < 25%   Drought frequencies high > 25%

The most benign for the US, and many places elsewhere, is a positive PDO and negative AMO that brings the Pacific rainfall east and the Atlantic rains southwards. Much of the south and west of America have above average rainfall leaving only a few dryer pockets to the north and west. Elsewhere, southern Europe and all of the Mediterranean have good rain, although parts of South East Asia will have droughts. These conditions were particularly prevalent from the late 1890s to 1914, and from 1976 to 1995.

With the AMO still negative and a negative PDO, the south and east of the US and the north-west has good rainfall, although the central states are hit by the impact of a cooler Pacific. Elsewhere, northern China and Central Asia have become unusually cool and dry with flooding to the south. Europe and the Mediterranean still have adequate rainfall. This was the pattern from 1916 to the early 1920s, and for the 1960s and the very early 1970s.

The combination of positive PDO and AMO gives rainfall to the west and Southwest, but the East Coast, particularly the Southeast, suffers from the rain belts moving north. This implies there is rain in California, the Southwest, Texas and the southern Mississippi. Outside the US, the rain belts will be further north in Europe making the Mediterranean dryer than usual. The western rim of the Pacific will suffer low rainfall in South East Asia but adequate precipitation in the north. These were the patterns from the late 1920s through the 1930s to the early 1940s. This combination was probably responsible for the dust bowl in a number of mid-Western states and the chaos associated with the rise of the warlords in China.

The most dangerous condition for the Americas, northern Asia, the Middle East and southern Europe is a negative PDO and a positive AMO. The PDO dries and cools the West and reduces North America's winter moisture, while the AMO leaves the interior of the continent dry and increases the risk of hurricanes along the East Coast. The wheat, corn and eastern cotton belts are left with less moisture and it is unusually dry in heavily populated California, Texas and Florida – America's primary fruit and vegetable growing areas.

Elsewhere, the positive AMO will bring drought conditions to the Mediterranean, including many parts of the Middle East. In the western Pacific, the areas most affected will be Northern China, Central Asia and much of the Middle East and Eastern Africa.

Depending upon the seriousness of the PDO, the following is a summary of how individual countries are likely to be affected.

Positive PDO, negative AMO

- *Benefiting*: North and South America, southern Europe, Northern China, Central Asia and the Middle East.

- *Suffering*: India and South East Asia.

Negative PDO, negative AMO

- *Benefiting*: Canada, the Pacific Northwest, Texas and the Southeast, the Midwest, South East Asia, Europe, the Eastern Mediterranean and India.

- *Suffering*: West Coast of the Americas, the Central Great Plains, South America, Northern China and Central Asia.

Positive PDO, positive AMO

- *Benefiting*: Southern central USA, California and Northern Europe,

- *Suffering*: Canada, remainder of USA, the Mediterranean, South East Asia, the Middle East and India.

Negative PDO, positive AMO

A condition likely to last into the third decade of the twenty-first century:

North America

As the rain belts move north around the Atlantic there is rain in the north-east and north-west but little in the Middle West and along the East Coast; this is badly affecting the crops in the interior. This reduced rainfall in the West will diminish the flow in the great Rio Grande and Colorado rivers serving southern California and the states bordering with Mexico.

Latin America

The west coast suffers from the rain belts moving west across the Pacific, with a likelyhood of reduced snow cover on the Andes that will diminish river flows on both sides of the range. Some parts of the eastern side will benefit from the tropics moving south, but others will suffer from desertification. Brazil has considerable water resources and has a great possibility for increasing grain supply in the longer term as the infrastructure is developed. Remember that Argentina had the fifth highest per capita GDP during the 1930s while the US was suffering from the dust bowl conditions.

Europe

Northern Europe and Russia will benefit from good rainfall. However, around the Mediterranean it will be unusually hot and dry, affecting primarily Spain, southern France, Italy and Greece. The region will also be subject to rising numbers of refugees from Africa.

Middle East

This region will become dry from both oscillations. This could cause conflicts (see Chapter 6) in the Middle East, which will have a similar rainfall to the 1970s but with 50% more population. Egypt could be badly affected from lower levels in Lake Victoria and abstractions upstream from the White Nile.

Indian subcontinent

This area should experience excellent monsoons, particularly to the east which could also be subject to flooding. This will not be true in Pakistan, which will be dryer then usual, and there will be concerns about control over the sources of the great rivers (see Chapter 7).

South East Asia

This area will experience excellent rainfall but much of this could be heavy and likely to cause frequent flooding.

Northern China

Northern China's main river is the Hwang Ho, the Yellow River, that some years barely reaches the sea, both from reduced flow from the source and from increased upstream abstraction. It is also heavily polluted, as are most Chinese rivers – 350,000 people die every year from foul water. The river delta is a main wheat growing area that will be severely affected as the flow lessens. China's control of many rivers is likely to impact on future conflicts.

Central Asia, Afghanistan and the Middle East

These have benefited from adequate moisture in the last thirty years where the population has increased rapidly, but the effect is likely to diminish as the rain belts are forced further south. There will be increased danger from conflicts and a rising tide of refugees. This pattern is shown diagrammatically opposite.

Diagram 3. Likely areas of drought with positive AMO and negative PDO

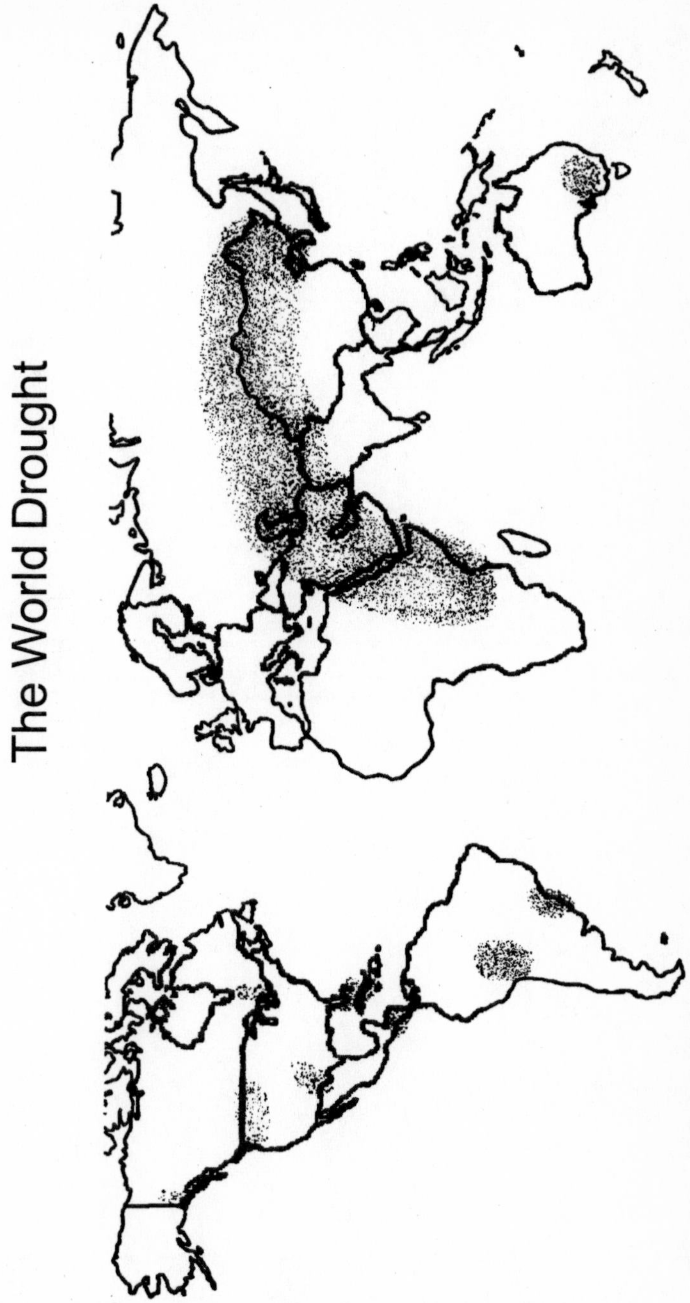

The World Drought

Source: Browning Newsletter

Longer term climatic cycle

A longer term climatic cycle was reported by the Browning Newsletter in December 2007, based on work done by the National Oceanic and Atmospheric Administration (NOAA). It seems that the tropics have been expanding since early in the nineteenth century caused by increased solar output, and are now nearer the poles by up to nearly 5 degrees of latitude – equivalent to 300 miles. This has forced the deserts, in particular, to move north and south. To the north, southern European countries will become increasingly dry, while in the Southern Hemisphere, south-east Australia is becoming dryer while the north-west will have added moisture.

The cycle, which is probably around 500 years in duration, explains why the Romans were able to grow grapes around the Tyne River in north-east England while Italy must have been exceptionally dry. Some 500 years later the Moors were able to colonise Spain and farm the land successfully for it resembled their home country. By 1492 the cycle had turned, the tropics were retreating and rain in Castille helped to support their troops who eventually removed the Muslims from Grenada.

Five hundred years later the cycle could be peaking around the year 2050 and the impact over time could be quite dramatic. Southern Europeans, and those living in south-east Australia, will have to learn to irrigate crops and to adapt to a hotter and dryer climate or move to areas of higher rainfall. It could also cause mass movements of people out of the marginal land of Mongolia and Manchuria towards Eastern Europe and south and west into China. This is a summary of how the cycle might affect different continents.

- **Europe** will be divided north and south. The south will become hotter and dryer, accentuating the effect of the warm Atlantic described earlier. As the north becomes warmer, countries like Russia will prosper and be able to grow more exotic crops that had previously been marginal. One can anticipate a drift of people northwards.

- **North America**, like Europe, will divide as the south becomes hotter and dryer while the north, including Canada, will become more temperate with warmer winters.

- The **Middle East** is likely to see an extension of Saudi deserts to the north, potentially affecting Iran, Iraq and probably Pakistan too.

- **Asia** will also become divided as Northern China and Central Asia become much dryer, accentuating the La Nina effect described earlier. To the south, South East Asia and India should see an increase in rainfall and become hotter.

- The **African Sahel** – that has been unusually dry could increase its rainfall, while deserts such as the Kalahari will move south threatening South Africa.

- **South America**, like Africa, will find an expansion of its tropical forests while the dry areas move south.

The crustal cycle

This is so-called because, as suggested earlier, the 180 years tidal cycle also creates tension in the earth. As we are now aware, the continents are in a state of perpetual drift, which means there are considerable areas where the oceanic crust is disappearing – mainly under the land masses – particularly around the Pacific. These destructive margins, as they are called, generate enormous tensions deep in the earth which, when triggered by external forces such as the moon's gravitational force, can release huge amounts of energy that cause earthquakes and volcanoes.

Shorter term there are lunar cycles. Although the sun's mass is infinitely greater than that of the moon, its gravitational effect is about one third that of the earth's satellite, which is directly responsible for the bi-monthly tidal rhythms. The greatest effect is when the earth, sun and moon are aligned at the time of a full or new moon, which causes unusually high tides, known as spring tides, on either sides of the earth that follow round as the earth rotates. This is the most usual time for seismic activity; neap tides occur when the moon is at 90 degrees to the earth-sun axis. These alignments also affect the atmosphere and the land on what are known as earth tides; these can cause seismic action whereby the earth can rise and fall up to 20 inches.

During these short-term cycles of around 18 years the moon nutates around the earth, causing it to move closer and further from the earth in its orbit. The closest point, known as the perigee, is due in 2010, but before this, in another orbit, the moon will be the closest to the earth that it has been for several hundred years from November 2007 to December 2008, with the most dangerous periods being the full and new moons. It is quite likely that the Sumatra and Pakistan earthquakes, both parts of the same tectonic plate, were an early harbinger of the disruption to the earth's crust that this will cause.

Earthquakes

Earthquakes are more common than volcanoes and, with the great increase in world population, are likely to cause increasingly local damage and loss of life. The one off Sumatra which caused the tsunami was unusual in that its epicentre was out at sea and its impact covered a very wide area of the Indian Ocean. In relatively modern times the next greatest loss of life after a tsunami followed the eruption of Krakatoa in 1883. It went off between Java and Sumatra and in those less populated days, caused the death of 60,000.

Volcanoes

The damage from a major eruption is often more widespread but usually less immediately destructive of life than a tsunami. A severe eruption would cause millions of tons of dust and acid to be discharged into the stratosphere which then spreads towards the poles. The impact is often quite dramatic for, when the sun is shielded, the temperature on earth falls, and as the poles become cooler the storm tracks are forced towards the equator. This denies moisture to many continental areas which disrupts food and living patterns.

To illustrate the power of volcanic eruptions in recent history, during late March/early April 1982, El Chichon exploded in Mexico's Chihas region with the force of a 10 megaton fusion bomb. The resulting dark cloud shielded sunlight from the earth and drifted north to halve the US corn crop and deplete the (then) Soviet harvest.

The next major one was Pinatubo, in Luzon in the Philippines, that erupted on June 15th 1991 with a similar force to El Chichon. It discharged 10 billion tonnes of magma and 20 million tons of sulphur dioxide and aerosols into the stratosphere – more than any other eruption since Krakatoa in 1883. This reduced temperatures by 1.1 degrees Fahrenheit in the Northern Hemisphere, making those in this region feel as though they were living over 300 miles further north.

As the debris drifted further north – taking three weeks to circle the earth – observers could see an orange cloud around the horizon that shielded the early and late sun. It cooled the circumpolar vortex which forced the rain belts further south, an effect that lasted several years before all the dust and sulphuric acid lattices eventually drifted into the troposphere and were dissipated. The areas primarily affected were the great continents which became unusually cool, and at times the cold weather in the US extended to the Mexican border.

The impact on crop yields was greater than that of El Chichon. Turkey was obliged to reduce the flow of the Euphrates into Syria and Iraq, which nearly precipitated a war. Elsewhere in the Middle East and Central Asia there were storms.

In April 2007, a relatively small eruption on the Kamchatka Peninsula by north-east Russia had the effect of sending a huge cold fist over much of North America that caused snow to fall on Los Angeles and Malibu beach. Other volcanoes cooled the polar vortex in the summer of 2007, which caused flooding in north-west Europe. But these are relatively small pinpricks; should a really major explosion occur in 2008 we have the example of Tambora – mentioned earlier. This reduced the global temperature by 2 or 3 degrees Fahrenheit, which, to those alive then, must have felt like living up to 1,000 miles closer to the poles; it had the effect of forcing the price of wheat in the US to over $6 a bushel – equivalent to several hundred dollars in today's money.

The latter half of the twentieth century was relatively clear of the eruptions that in earlier years had created the sort of weather patterns described earlier. This has meant that mankind has adjusted to building close to the seashore and in areas closer to the flood plains something that would have been unthinkable many decades earlier. They have also located on areas of high potential seismic activity and built near to volcanoes, which could prove highly dangerous should the tectonic plates be subject to unusually large stresses.

If the planetary cycles are to work as they have in the past, very considerable adjustment will have to be made to the way we live. The next chapters deal with at least some of the implications.

References

- www.nature.com/news/2004/041025/full/news041025-15.html

- www.paztcn.wr.usgs.gov/rsch_highlight/articles/200404.html

- CIA Factbook.geo

- *Browning Newsletter*, The Frazer Publishing Co. PO Box 494, Burlington, Vermont 05402

- *Climate and Food Security*, by The American Foundation (International Rice Institute, 1989)

- *Encyclopedia Britannica*

- *Future Storm*, by William Houston and Robin Griffiths (Harriman House, 2006)

- *Riding the Business Cycle*, by William Houston (Little, Brown, 1995)

- www.sesfoundation.org

- www.StrategicReview.com, October 12th 2006

- *When The Rivers Run Dry*, by Fred Pearce (Beacon Press, 2006)

- www.halkinservices.co.uk, Weekly Letter, October 12th 2006

2

Water Circulation and Conservation

This chapter is about the nuts and bolts of water; how it arrives, circulates, is treated and is used. There is a section on dams and their contribution to greenhouse gases, and of particular interest is how Israeli water technology could make a major contribution to global peace.

Water is the most abundant substance on earth, with the seas containing over 97% of the water on the planet. Its presence in the oceans, atmosphere and on land makes it possible to live on earth because it retains heat in the atmosphere and on the ground, without which habitation would be impossible. It acts as the medium for heat and moisture transfer, and it allows us to live in areas that would otherwise be uninhabitable. The quantity of water on the planet has remained constant for over 4 billion years.

The molecule of this extraordinary substance is made up of two atoms of hydrogen bonding with one atom of oxygen – two of the most reactive gases uniting to form a stable molecule. However, water molecules have free polarities enabling them to bond with others, and these bonds can only be broken with the application of heat or an electric current. Water has the unusual capacity to exist in a solid, liquid or vaporous state; it requires heat for moving upwards from liquid to vapour, needing what is known as latent heat to change its state. This capacity enables heat to be transferred through the agent of wind streams and the gyroscopic Coriolis force, from the tropics to more temperate zones.

Water is one of the best naturally occurring solvents, making it ideal for washing and the transfer of waste. Its capacity to absorb oxygen – particularly at low temperatures – enables it to maintain life in the rivers, lakes and oceans, and to readily oxidise organic pollution. This quality of absorption makes it possible for plants to transfer essential elements from the earth through their roots. To make use of this, plants absorb carbon dioxide under the influence of sunlight and give off oxygen – a factor seemingly not taken into account by some global warming aficionados. Water together with carbon dioxide forms a weak acid that drives the rock cycle – a multi-million year process of denuding minerals from the surface which are eventually returned to the earth through magma.

As suggested earlier, the capacity to exist in three states drives the hydrological cycle that carries water evaporated from the oceans to the atmosphere and then to the land, where it falls as precipitation. If where it falls is hot enough, over 90% is evaporated back into the atmosphere leaving only some 7% to run-off and 3% to be absorbed as ground water; in more temperate climates only two thirds is evaporated leaving behind a higher proportion as run-off or to be retained in the soil.

A major problem for life is that less than 3% of all water is fresh and of the total over 2.75% is tied up in the ice caps and groundwater, leaving a very small percentage immediately available in lakes and rivers; polar melting would add only 2% to the oceans. The distribution of the climatic belts and man's ability to extract groundwater have been major factors in supporting a rising world population. One might possibly live in temperate latitudes without oil, but it is impossible to exist without water.

For this we are helped enormously by the tilted axis of the earth: that is at 23½ degrees to the plane of the ecliptic – the passage of our planet around the sun. During the course of a year in the Northern Hemisphere, the rain belts move south in the winter and north in the summer bringing rain to the great plains of Canada, the breadbasket of the Ukraine and, in its southern phase, to the Antipodes and southern latitudes. The seasons have brought to the temperate latitudes an energy to work in winters and the essential requirement of providing enough food to store for the winter – a need somewhat reduced by globalisation.

To comprehend the circulation of water we are obliged to consider something about hydrology – that is the study of the supply, conservation and movement of water.

The atmosphere contains 10% more water in vapour form than all the rivers and lakes in the world where it is the major component, constituting 95% of the greenhouse gases. Of the pure gases, nitrogen constitutes 78% oxygen 21%, and leaving little for the other gases such as argon, methane and carbon dioxide. These are mostly contained in the lower 60 miles nearest to the earth where the air is turbulent and of this, the lowest 10 miles are the most significant for deciding our weather.

Precipitation

Precipitation is caused by water vapour in the atmosphere condensing on reaching cooler air when it coalesces around tiny dust particles that are always present. Once this reaches a critical mass it overcomes the natural updraft in the air and falls as rain under the force of gravity; hail or snow is formed if the air temperature is freezing.

There are several ways the air can be cooled; usually the warm/moist sub-tropical air travelling towards the poles meets a cooler polar airstream to force the warm air higher into cooler regions. Higher ground is another reason for air being pushed upwards for the rain to fall on the windward side leaving the lee side dryer. When there is a temperature inversion (the air warming, not cooling as it rises) Cumulo-nimbus clouds provide a powerful upwards airstream often generating thunderstorms, freezing rain and hail. Hydrology is concerned with methods of assessing the measurement of rainfall and snow cover on a wide spread of surfaces.

There are numerous ways of measuring the degree of precipitation through the use of rain gauges which need to be adapted to the ground cover, whether it is liquid, bare earth, urban, or some form of vegetation. This is important because before building a reservoir a study must analyse a number of seasons to generate a representative input. Then there is the question of evaporation, through which most of the rainfall is lost.

Evaporation

Evaporation happens when water is present and there is energy available from the sun, the residual warmth of the earth, or elsewhere, to apply enough latent heat to turn moisture into vapour. In addition, growing vegetation loses moisture in the process of photosynthesis and transpiration. These combined are termed *evotranspiration* (ET), but there are a number of additional factors.

- There must be an **abundant supply of moisture**, which is why the highest evaporation takes place over the seas, rivers and lakes. Other types of surface release moisture at different rates. For example, sandy soil, through which water can percolate easily, has a higher rate than clay. If ET on bare earth is taken as one, then vegetation has varying degrees of moisture loss with pasture having a factor of three and many trees nine.

- Evaporation can only take place where the surrounding air is not already saturated, which is why **wind** is important. A windless day may allow a moisture barrier to build up near the surface which reduces evaporation, while a windy day will increase ET, even in winter.

- The **seasons** are important because aquifers become full when there is very little evaporation in winter. In semi-tropical regions, the very high evaporation in summer makes irrigation an essential factor in food production. This in turn becomes a danger when water, pumped from aquifers, becomes salty and this is retained on the surface, destroying the capacity of the land to grow crops – an increasing problem where land is irrigated.

Run-off and retention

Moisture then has two options: it can either *run-off* or be *retained* as groundwater: again, several factors apply.

- Roughened soil provides the best surface for water retention, helped by vegetation and mulch. Crops such as tubers promote absorption and unploughed set-aside helps run-off. The best infiltration is found under trees – particularly oaks.

- The upper layer of soil is known as the aeration zone, from which ET takes place. Below this is the zone of saturation, with the dividing line being the top of the water table. Water percolates through capillary, osmosis or electrostatic action until an area is saturated. This is known as the field capacity.

- The majority of water in streams comes from the surface of the ground and groundwater – the latter taking ten times as long to arrive. More recently, groundwater has added pollution to streams and rivers from chemical additives, which has led to demands for less harmful fertilisers, and controls on industrial effluent.

- Snow is the best cover. First the albedo (or heat reflection) reduces transpiration, then the plants and crops below are protected from damaging sub-zero temperatures. Finally, rain usually provides the melting agent, adding trickling moisture and warmth; vapour gives out latent heat as it condenses.

Precipitation, evaporation, retention and run-off are usually in balance depending upon the surface. Grassland reduces ET but retention falls; in woodland the effect is reversed. The next question is the control of run-off because nearly two thirds, after evaporation, becomes flood water. This is most evident with monsoons, or in more recent times, when flooding filled the Prague metro, and there was devastation in 2007 in France and England; at these times the jet stream was stationary over these areas. In more controlled regions, the aim is to retain excess water in dams, reservoirs, locks and sluices.

Water stress is estimated from the percentage of the run-off that needs to be captured. Countries using less than 5% have few problems, those in the 10%-20% bracket have increasing difficulties. Those needing in excess of 20% have a major issue that affects national development. For example, India is presently using half the water available, the balance coming from groundwater. By 2025 it is estimated that 92% will be needed – an almost impossible target. Another area that has increasing water problems is Northern China (see Chapter 7). Run-off is an important factor in planning where to install reservoirs.

In most developed countries a great deal is known from recorded data about the hydrographic balance – essential before planning a reservoir or a dam. The lack of this data in some less developed countries has led to several poor decisions for citing dams. There are also climatic shifts described in the previous chapter that have been present for thousands of years which affect the hydrological balance; the shifting rain belts often deprive areas expecting precipitation and deluge others. As suggested earlier, volcanic action generates, for a period, unusual climatic and precipitation patterns.

Controlling, preserving and using water

Hydrologists have some answers to controlling water excesses, as the Dutch have demonstrated with their complex systems of dams, storm barriers, sluices and channels to control the vast complex of waterways at the mouth of the Rhine. Elsewhere, Canada is one of the few countries with an abundance of water that has attracted great projects around James Bay and the Mackenzie River Basins. On a smaller scale, several rivers have been modified against storm surges by using barriers, increased levees, overflow basins or diversions. One of the most popular means of retention is to build a barrier.

Dams

Blocking river water stretches back as far back as the sixth millennium BC – about the same time as irrigation was first used. But the use of dams to control water has met with mixed success, particularly in developing countries.

Evaporation

In his book, *When The Rivers Run Dry*, Fred Pearce reports an incredible statistic that the Aswan High Dam loses between 10 and 13 million acre-feet of water every year, – an amount equivalent to the total amount running from taps in England over the same time period. And evaporation losses are not confined to Africa. Dams or reservoirs in the southern states of North America, such as Lake Elephant Butte on the Rio Grande, or Lakes Meade and Powell on the Colorado River, lose 6 feet a year; like most dammed rivers this is equivalent to losing a tenth or more of the river flow.

On a global scale a Russian hydrologist has estimated that 285 million acre-feet is lost every year through evaporation: 40% is lost in Asia, a quarter in Africa and a sixth in North America. He calculated that 20 million people in Australia lose the equivalent of 53,000 gallons a head. But this is not the only problem.

Population displacement

Building dams displace a very large number of people, many of them farmers, and the land is lost permanently to agriculture, as the loess is normally spread as a fertiliser when a river like the Nile floods. As the reservoirs become progressively full of silt the water capacity is lost, and some dams have had to be abandoned and new ones built, if convenient sites can be found. Apart from disappearing farmland, ancient cities in countries like China have gone forever, as have many species. But there have been unforeseen results.

Greenhouse gases

In Brazil it has been discovered that rotten submerged vegetation produces methane, a greenhouse gas with a toxicity 17 times that of carbon dioxide – equivalent to an equivalent fossil fuel power plant. **As each dam has been built over a valley it is estimated that the total methane produced is equivalent to more than all aircrafts' carbon footprints in a year**. It is ironical that small countries with dams now must be considered as producers of greenhouse gases along with nations using conventional power plants. There is also the problem of flood control.

Flood control

One of the arguments for dams is the control of flooding, but this runs counter to other requirements such as providing enough head for hydro-electric generation. The level cannot be so finely judged to have the added capacity to avoid a downstream flood. Although spillways can remove some of the excesses, the construction of some dams are themselves causing concern.

In half a century 322 Chinese dams had failed – including the world's greatest disaster. In August 1975, the 400-foot Banqiao Dam in the Henan Province failed when a typhoon hit the hills behind and the Ru River sent a torrent of water that overcame the structure and another downstream. The flood formed a wall of water 7 miles wide and 20 feet high that caused a death toll variously estimated at between 80,000 and 200,000 people.

Water deficits in hot countries where the rate of evaporation and run-offs are very high, presents a problem of ownership when much of the moisture cannot be absorbed; this then often becomes a matter of dispute over the question of riparian rights over a whole river basin (see below).

Territorial sovereignty

There are conflicting principles of territorial sovereignty over water resources. On the one side there is the *Harmon Doctrine* that claims rights for upstream users. By contrast, the principle of *Absolute Territorial Integrity* holds that no nation may use its resources to the detriment of a downstream state. This is extended by the *Principle of Condominium* or common jurisdiction that holds the rights of a state are strictly limited and the prior consent from other interested states is needed before water developments can take place. This is enforced by the *Principle of Equitable Utilisation* which holds that developments are permissible if they do not harm the resources of a neighbour.

These factors are mostly written into arrangements between parties in the developed world, but there are exceptions in the Middle East, Asia and Africa, where many countries share common catchment basins. For example, the Beas-Sutlej and Ravi rivers in Pakistan both pass through the Indian Punjab before flowing into Pakistan. Other examples are set out in Chapters 6 and 7 and have often been the source of conflicts.

This is true also of aquifers that water huge areas of grain production on the North China Plain, the Punjab, the Indus Basin and the Great Plains of the US. Coupled with other factors, described later, these could run dry or be threatened by the climatic shifts described in Chapter 1. These sources of groundwater can be very extensive and can occur at various depths in such permeable rock as limestone, where often vast underground caverns have gathered water from subterranean streams. Typical areas are the Atlas Mountains, ranges in Lebanon, Syria, Israel, parts of the Sierra Nevada, Beijing, Bangkok and the US Midwest.

One of the largest aquifers in the world is called the Ogallala Formation that covers several US states including the Texas Panhandle, Kansas, Nebraska and some adjoining territories. The area covers over 583,000 square kilometres and in some places is 300 metres deep. Initially it was fed from rivers draining the Rockies and crossing the High Plains, but many of these now flow elsewhere.

The area is extensively farmed using pumped water, but the problem is that it is not being replenished fast enough to make up the shortfall; studies have shown there is a net depletion in all the associated states except for Nebraska and South Dakota – Texas and Kansas having the highest usage.

Agreement over the control of aquifers in the Middle East is one of the critical matters for a settlement there (see below and Chapter 6).

Distributing and husbanding water

Irrigation is essential to cultivation in mainly hot regions; 68% of these are in Asia, 17% in North America, 9% in Europe and only 5% in Africa. This is up to 40% of the total acreage tilled and is likely to be a large proportion of the land forecast to be taken out of production in the years to 2020 through salination and other factors (see Chapter 3). The other problem is that by 2030 many countries in the Middle East and North Africa will be using 60% of their renewable water resources, compared to 40% at present.

The most simple and widely used method of watering crops is by allowing water to cover an area, or more selectively flow along furrows or borders where it permeates the rest of the field – this is known as *basin flood irrigation*. Although easy to manage and cheap to operate, this method suffers from the obvious flaws of wasting well over half the water through evaporation or uncontrolled run-off. It is for this reason that more sophisticated methods have been devised in more developed countries.

One of these methods is to sprinkle water where and when it is needed, either centrally through high-powered rotating jets or through what is known as *wheel line irrigation*. Here, a series of wheels supporting a long sprinkler bar is arrayed on one side of a field, hoses are connected and the specific area watered for a timed period; the hoses are then disconnected, the whole structure moved on and the process repeated. Probably the most sophisticated method of water distribution pioneered by Israeli farmers is *trickle irrigation*, whereby underground pipes deliver the precise quantity of water and nutrients at pre-arranged times to each plant, shrub or tree (see the case study later in the chapter).

Engineers can also contribute to water saving by devising systems for reducing leaks in old water mains where, on average, a quarter or more, of the water available is lost – around London the loss is nearer one third. Old installations can either be paralleled to relieve the mains pressure or pipes laid within the originals. Other downstream measures include water-saving domestic appliances, smaller cisterns, installing water meters, and recycling unpolluted grey domestic water for flushing lavatories and watering gardens.

Regenerating water

Waste water

The treatment of waste water has enabled the growth of cities that could otherwise not have had access to fresh water or be able to dispose of waste. Where this has been neglected, such as in many parts of China, increasing numbers are dying from water-borne diseases and pollution, which force people towards regions where it will be safer to live.

Modern sewage plants have to cope with a wide variety of domestic and industrial waste. They may also have to deal with surface water via drains that, through flooding, can often overwhelm systems and lead to the discharge of raw sewage; for this reason the surface water is usually dealt with separately.

Before Victorian times it was usual for human and household (mainly organic) effluent to be discharged directly into rivers, lakes and estuaries. This created the most terrible smell – it is said that the fetid air around the House of Commons led to the funding for London's sewers. The sewers also helped the survival of the fish that had been denied oxygen which was previously needed to break down the effluent.

In due course the new sewage system derived a measure of primary pollution known as BOD5 (five-day biological oxygen demand) – the amount of oxygen extracted from water by bacteria when pollutants are decomposed. There is also a secondary pollution, which is the demand for oxygen stimulated by the fertilisation of the natural water plant life. Sewage is rich in nitrogen, phosphorous and potassium, all excellent fertilisers, which is why the secondary demand for oxygen is around five times the primary.

The effluent, in turn, is broken down into black and greywater:

- *black water* is the effluent from lavatories and constitutes from one third to half the total;

- *greywater* is the waste from baths, washing, kitchens and so on, that is likely to become increasingly treated and re-circulated near the source.

However, sewage treatment has to deal with industrial and domestic use, so the process has to be more extensive than just oxygenation.

1. Primary treatment includes the removal of fats, oils, and greases that are lighter than water and can be skimmed off. The solids are sand, gravel and stones – referred to as grits. These are all passed though mechanical screens, the grits are allowed to settle and are then removed.

2.   The next stage is designed substantially to degrade the biological content primarily from human, food and detergent waste. It uses a similar technique to natural cleansing by spraying the polluted water through oxygen-rich aggregates on which bacteria are allowed to grow. There are many variants on this secondary treatment.

3.   The final stage, sometimes called *effluent polishing*, passes the water through oxygen-rich water to remove final bacteria, filters to remove residual solids, and often uses light chlorination as a disinfectant. It is then discharged into rivers for the next cycle of use.

This process is typical of developed countries, but in the developing world the bulk of domestic and industrial waste water is discharged without treatment, or just with primary filtration. **In Latin America only 15% of collected waste water is treated; in China the figure is reported to be 45%, but even so 350,000 people died of water pollution in 2006.** In these countries water has to be boiled to make it potable. This has extremely serious implications for water-borne diseases such as diarrhoea, typhus and cholera, for half of the world's population who live in some 24 cities (the diseases are covered in more detail in Chapter 5). Specialists argue that due to the low reliability of water treatment plants, the first priority in these areas should be investment in basic hygiene before more expensive solutions are considered.

Greywater

The case for greywater treatment plants arises directly from conditions set out earlier in this chapter: that living will only become possible when water is conserved and used wisely. By mid 2007, a number of units were running in Sweden and the US – either where water is expensive or there is motivation to grow plants or vegetables, or to conserve water. This is a brief description of the system.

About one third of all domestic water is used to flush lavatories, which means that it is unusual for it to be re-used directly in developed countries; this is not true in the East where discharge is often used as 'night soil'. However, this does not mean that all water cannot be re-circulated.

Of the 150 litres/person/day used in the UK (this figure is nearer 380 litres/day in parts of the US), around 100 litres/day can be recycled from bathing, washing, cleaning and so on. Apart from organic matter, greywater contains a high proportion of nitrogen (that is notoriously difficult to remove but is a good fertiliser), fewer pathogens from the exclusion of faeces, and a higher concentration of oxygen. This implies a much simpler treatment process.

Most greywater treatment plants consist firstly of a pre-treatment filter where solids can settle as in a septic tank, there is then a filter to remove solids in suspension, and finally a planter bed. The latter replicates conditions in water where micro-organisms reduce the organic content. The resultant water may not be directly potable but can be used for flushing lavatories and for watering the garden. A typical installation in a cool climate is where vegetables may be grown in a greenhouse irrigated by recovered greywater and warmed by the heat from the degeneration process.

Desalination

Desalination (covered more extensively in Chapter 8) is a process for removing salt from sea or brackish (0.05-3% salt) water; part-removal makes it suitable for irrigation or animal consumption, total removal for domestic use. **There are some 2500 desalination plants running in the world**, the largest being at Jebel Ali in the UAE producing 300 million cubic meters of water a year, and there is one for Riyadh generating nearly 2.3 million litres a day. Other plants are elsewhere in the Middle East, the Caribbean and increasingly in the US, Singapore, Spain, Australia, China and so on.

Engineers have devised a number of methods for extracting fresh water from salt water but these are expensive, costing from 4 to 10 times as much as water from a dam. There may also be problems in discharging the brine back into the oceans, as this can have a damaging effect on sea life. There are at least four methods:

1. **Solar power** is widely used for heating in warm climates and increasingly as a pre-heater in temperate areas. Solar radiation is also used for distillation with nothing more complicated than seawater covered by a greenhouse-like structure that condenses and collects the fresh water.

2. **Refrigeration** at a reduced pressure is used to expel impurities. Once frozen, fresh water is extracted from the ice and vapour.

3. The most usual method is through **distillation** where, after filtration, seawater is boiled at reduced pressure to lessen the heat used. The distillate is often passed through the feed-water pre-heater of a power plant, which is usually built in parallel. There may be several stages run in sequence depending upon the purity of water needed.

4. The **reverse osmosis technique** that uses less heat, but more electrical energy, pumps saline water through a membrane that removes the salt and the process is continued in successive stages until the water is at acceptable salinity.

A case study

Long before the state of Israel was formed in 1948, Jewish settlements had started either as *kibbutzim*, where everything was held in common, or a *moshav*, a co-operative village where individual households worked their land while buying and selling together. These groups set about reclaiming land that had fallen out of production over the centuries from deforestation, soil erosion, salination and neglect. Rocky fields were cleared, terraces were built on hills, swamplands were drained, trees planted and salt washed off the land. Since 1948, the area under cultivation has grown from 165,000 hectares to around 435,000 ha, and the number of agricultural communities increased from 400 to 900, including a number of Arab villages. During this time agriculture has increased 16 times, some 3 times the rate of population growth.

It is estimated that by 2020 Israel's population will have grown over 40% to 8.5 million, but only half the amount of fresh water will be allocated to agriculture; at the same time the land available for farming will have declined by 18% due to urban expansion. This is a tall order for any country, but it is intended to meet this target by first of all increasing the numbers employed on the land. They will then switch production from crops such as cotton to growing fruit, vegetables and higher added-value produce. Israel's agriculture derives an export surplus allowing it to import much of its grain, oilseeds, meat, fish, sugar, coffee and cocoa.

This is how they plan to achieve this result:

Water conservation

Water conservation has been the key to Israel's farming success. With 60% of the country either arid or semi-arid, rainfall (an average of 28 inches in the north per annum and around two inches in the south) conservation and recycling becomes key. With rain falling between November and April, several large firms have specialised in conservation, irrigation and filtration equipment.

In a partnership between science and the industry, agricultural output has increased almost fivefold without additional water in the last 30 years. This has been achieved by:

1. **Selecting and breeding crops** that need less moisture and importing crops that have been successfully grown in countries such as Australia, Asia and Africa.

2. Introducing extensive **drip irrigation** (described earlier) with covered pipes to reduce evaporation. More recent innovations are designed to spread and retain moisture even more efficiently.

3. **Hydroponics**. This is a greenhouse system where plants such as vegetables are grown in precisely the correct carbon dioxide-rich atmosphere and with nutrients and water sprayed at programmed intervals at the roots.

4. An extensive **aquifer** of brackish water has been discovered in the Negev that will enable specialised crops to be grown. This and the Arava areas now

produce 40% of all vegetables and 90% of all the melons. Olive groves fed with brackish water have already achieved a six-fold output compared with normally watered trees.

5.   **Desalination** plants are being constructed.

Mechanisation

Mechanisation has increased yields as part of the Green Revolution in many countries, but Israel has developed the idea by designing heavy-duty tilling equipment, planting, harvesting and transplanting equipment as well as the irrigation plant described earlier.

Innovation

Innovation will continue to be an essential programme for the future where, for example, a kilogram of hybrid tomato seeds may sell for $7,000 compared to the same weight of tomatoes selling for around $5. All sectors will be covered where, in a land with little grazing, specialist fodder has generated excellent milk yields and fish farming has created higher outputs by oxygenation of the water and beneficial feed. In agriculture there is a move away from mass-produced crops to intensive growing of niche species such as hybrid, virus-resistant tomatoes or cultured banana tree saplings; grapes are now grown with brackish water in desert conditions.

References

- *Diapason Commodities Management*, Lausanne, Switzerland and London

- *Engineering & Technology*, December 2007 (IET, Faraday House, Six Hills Way, Stevenage SG1 2AY, UK)

- *Fundamentals of Hydrology*, by Tim Davie (Routledge 2003)

- *Future Storm*, by William Houston and Robin Griffiths (Harriman House 2006)

- *Global Hydrology*, by J. A. A. Jones (Longman's 1997)

- *History of the Decline and Fall of the Roman Empire*, by Edward Gibbon (Penguin Classics, 2000)

- Jewish Virtual Library – Israeli Agriculture: Coping with Growth

- MEMRI, *The Looming Crisis of Water in the Middle East,* by Dr Nimrod Raphael

- *Riding the Business Cycle*, by William Houston (Little, Brown, 1995)

- *Seeds of Change*, by Henry Hobhouse (Sidgwick and Jackson 1985)

- *Water: The International Crisis*, by Robin Clarke (Earthscan Publications, 1991)

- *When The Rivers Run Dry*, by Fred Pearce (Beacon Press, 2006)

- www.wikipedia.com

- *What is Food Security and Famine and Hunger?*, by Melaku Ayalew (www.Bradford.ac.uk/Research)

- www.greywater.com

3

The Coming Food Deficit

Summary

The Green Revolution dominated the post-war period for growing food. By providing cultivars suitable for particular climates, improving cultivation, encouraging irrigation and through wide use of fertilisers, the output enabled the global population to grow exponentially. Plentiful food helped to raise living standards in many parts of the world, and instead of a diet of rice or cassava, meat and fish were now in demand.

This bonanza is now coming to an end through the advent of shifting ocean climatic profiles, over-pumped aquifers, saline pollution of the soil, erosion of the topsoil and increasing desertification. This has meant increasing competition to grow the most advantageous crops on the good arable land; it can only lead to a spiral in food prices. The process becomes more serious because the consumption of water has quadrupled in the last 50 years.

As up to 40% of food output is irrigated, the most vulnerable parts of the world with major centres of population are now facing drought, and possibly starvation too. Should this happen, millions of people will be displaced and, in the worst case, this toxic mix could hit nations armed with nuclear weapons.

Introduction

The ocean oscillations described in Chapter 1, and shown in Diagram 3, describe the major areas of potential deficiency and abundance; Chapters 4 and 5 show how this is likely to impact on people's behaviour and those displaced through drought.

Many of those who had the expectation of abundant water to drink and grow crops are likely to have a severe deficit; those expecting adequate rainfall could be flooded for years until the third decade of the new century, when the ocean oscillations become more beneficial.

We can now evaluate the areas that should have adequate water to feed themselves:

> North America, northern Europe, Australasia, Anatolia, South America, India, Southern China and South East Asia.

Those areas with a water deficit are likely to be:

> Northern China, Central Asia, Pakistan, the Middle East, East Africa, and the Mediterranean.

This pattern could be seriously affected should a large volcanic eruption seriously cool the polar vortex and reduce global temperatures. Experience shows this would act like a broad icy 'finger' pointing down from the Arctic Circle to make parts of the great northern continents difficult to live in. As oceans heat up and cool less quickly than the land masses, those bordering the oceans will be less affected. These 'fingers' will create extreme cold and cause serious water shortages in:

- Russia, Central Asia, Canada, Northern China, the Mid West, and Central and Eastern Europe.

- Because of the likely reduced snow cover, rivers flowing from the Rockies, Himalayas, Nepal and portions of the Andes will have reduced snowmelt in the spring. This will be felt particularly by the Colorado, Missouri and Rio Grande in the US, the Yellow River in China, and the Indus and Ganges in the subcontinent.

These areas would find it progressively difficult to grow crops and the bitter cold would force people to move – as they have done for many centuries in the past.

Vulnerability of crops

The Green Revolution mentioned earlier had a dramatic impact on growing crops. For example, while 14 million tons of chemicals were spread during the 1950s, this rose to 150 million tons later in the century. Overuse of land has meant that only one third of the humus is being replaced in the US; globally, it is estimated that 30% will have been lost by 2020.

This has had a dramatic impact on many countries' ability to grow food, as shown in Diagram 4. The global production of cereals reached a peak in 1998, then declined nearly 40% until 2006, although demand continued to rise and output has become more volatile. The second chart complements this, showing how in the years from 1998 to 2006, the output was in deficit for six out of the seven years.

Diagram 4. The growth and reduction of global carry-over stocks

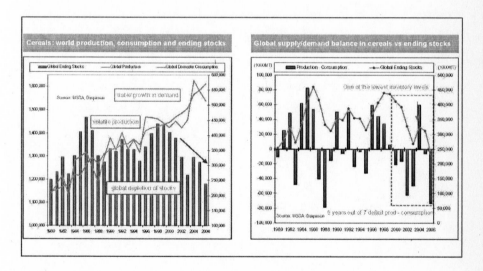

Source: Diapason

Total global cropland is around 1.5 billion hectares and most is currently in production. However, up to one third is being steadily eroded from increased desertification, topsoil reduction, salinity and used-up aquifers and will be out of production by 2020. However, the impact could be somewhat neutralised by making arable land in Russia and elsewhere, more productive.

Diapason reports that 1 billion hectares would be needed to make up the balance. As up to 40% of food production is irrigated, this loss of output will be felt primarily by countries in Asia, Africa and the Middle East – areas that have seen the greatest increase in population.

Sources of possible relief

The sources of possible relief imply a much greater degree of self-control and understanding if the present decline in arable land is to be arrested – let alone reversed. These are some well-tried disciplines.

Reverse top-soil erosion

Reverse top-soil erosion by planting trees on areas cleared by logging, often for firewood, in many areas of Africa and Asia; excessive grazing will have had the same effect. Not only has the topsoil been washed away into rivers but the silt has reduced the downstream depth and increased the danger of flooding. For example, Robin Clarke reports that the Cherrapunji region of India has one of the highest recorded rainfalls in the world during the monsoon season. However for 25 years, the region has been devastated by reckless grazing and logging, rendering it almost impossible to retain water.

The cleared areas should be planted with grass and trees to retain what topsoil is left and the process of adding humus can begin, although it will be generations before the land is fit for growing cereals light grazing can take place sooner. This is a long-term programme and is vital to avoid future generations from starving.

Reduced run-off and improved water retention

Reduced run-off and improved water retention has been brilliantly achieved in Israel, whose farmers are extremely aware of water conservation. As suggested in the previous chapter, improving water retention by planting trees will help, as will digging tanks to take some of the rainfall that would otherwise be wasted. In hot climates these can be fed from wadis that receive only occasional storms.

Reducing urban usage

Reducing urban usage is practised in many hot countries where houses are built over small reservoirs for domestic and garden use. The greywater can then be treated by filtering out the solids and re-oxygenating the remainder for flushing lavatories, watering gardens or in agriculture. By 1990, some 30% of all domestic water in Israel was recycled to farms, which has the added advantage of returning nitrogen to the soil; it was planned to raise this figure to nearer 80% by 2000. In the process, pollution in streams and at coasts has been considerably reduced.

Intelligent irrigation

Intelligent irrigation, as practiced by informed countries, considerably reduces water waste (see Chapter 2).

Clearing saline soil

Clearing saline soil is a considerable undertaking involving heavy equipment to break up the salt crust, which is then removed and replaced with fresh topsoil. At the same time adequate drains need to be dug and the new soil periodically washed with fresh water.

Bringing water to remote villages

Bringing water to remote villages where it has to be carried over a distance is an important advance for communities that would otherwise wither. Even pedal-driven pumps and covered storage tanks are an advantage.

Developing hybrids that can use substandard water

Developing hybrids that can use substandard water has been extensively researched in Israel (see case study in Chapter 2), but this subject covers the whole area of genetically modified crops (GM). It can be said that the whole process of adaptation has been the subject of unscientific modification for centuries, but came into greater scrutiny towards the end of the nineteenth century when Scotland and Sweden experimented with breeding a hybrid of wheat and rye called triticale. The former has gluten, essential for making bread, while rye can withstand lower temperatures and is more resistant to drought; the major growers are Poland and Scandinavia with their harsher growing conditions.

The process was taken a stage further around the 1920s by Henry Wallace (later a vice president to Franklin D. Roosevelt). He had been brought up on a farm in Iowa and experimented with breeding high-yielding strains of corn adapted to different growing conditions; he started Pioneer Hi-Bred, which went on to become a major agricultural supplier.

GM takes the process to the next logical stage. Instead of producing hybrids in the field this is now done in a laboratory by modifying the DNA to produce particularly resistant strains. The first product was a tomato with rotting-resistant qualities. Next was insect-repellent cotton and then a soybean resistant to herbicides. By 2005, 222 million acres had been planted with GM crops, over 55% in the US but also in Brazil, Argentina, India and China.

Bearing in mind the history of plant adaptation, it seems strange there is such resistance to GM crops in Europe, despite no health hazards being experienced in the US and elsewhere. The main opposition seems to come from those concerned about the ecosystem, where insect-killing strains will mean less food further up the chain. Yet others produce reports showing that GM crops reduce yield – particularly in unusual conditions of drought and others show that the plant-attacking insects are now mutating into more belligerent strains. The arguments will continue, but in the final analysis the decision will be made whether GM crops can thrive in the difficult conditions outlined in this book.

Growing high added-value food

Following Israel's lead by growing high added-value food to pay for imports from the relatively few countries likely to have surpluses.

Each of these factors would help to stop and even reverse the degradation of arable land, but few of the techniques described will need anything other than a long-term implementation. In the Afterword we suggest how people in the West should be used to introduce the remedies as part of an important educational and practical plan. We now consider how individual crops could help improve food production.

Major crops

The main crops grown to feed the world's growing population are wheat, corn/maize, rice, and possibly barley.

Wheat

Wheat is the most important global crop planted in many countries, having been first cultivated domestically from 3,000 BC, probably in Turkey. It is a sturdy cereal able to prosper with only ten inches of rain a year and in relatively low temperatures. Of the millions of hectares under general cultivation in the world, 15% is given over to wheat which generated a total output of 626 million tonnes in 2005. The major growers are: China with 96mt, India 72mt, USA 57mt and Russia 46mt. Other major producers are: Ukraine, France, Australia, Canada, Kazakhstan and Turkey. As a ton of wheat needs 1,000 tons of rainwater, probably only India, France and Turkey could be unaffected by the climatic shifts described earlier – although the former already has severe water problems.

Unfortunately, the **output of wheat peaked around 1980 and has since declined by an eighth**, as shown in Diagram 5, reflecting the reduction of arable land now taking place. This continued into 2007, when Canada's output, the second largest exporter, showed a further decline. The shortfall will be of major concern to developing countries whose staple fare is this grain, eaten either as bread or cereal.

In the West a good proportion is used as animal feed, with the remainder consumed as bread, breakfast food, cakes, and so on. Of all crops, wheat is likely to prove the most durable in the difficult years ahead.

Barley

Barley was the most important crop of the ancient Egyptians, grown for a form of bread and beer. It is now primarily grown in Europe for beer, cakes, biscuits and animal feed. Although a relatively fragile plant easily damaged by heavy rain showers, it has the advantage of adapting to slightly brackish water. The prime growers in 2005 were: at Russia 16.7mt, Canada 12.1mt, Germany 11.7mt and France 10.4mt. As Diagram 5 shows, it has the same deteriorating output profile as wheat.

Diagram 5. Output profile of Wheat and Barley from 1960 to the present

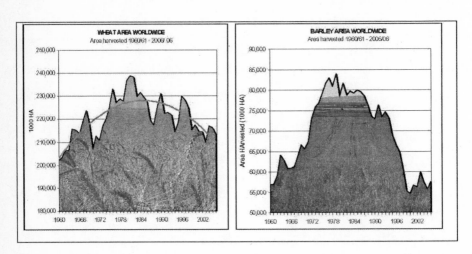

Source: Diapason

Rice

Rice is a highly plentiful crop, and the staple food of nearly one half of the world's population, particularly in China, East and South East Asia. It was probably first cultivated in the Indus basin some 7,000 years ago, from where it spread south and east. Of the 700 million tonnes produced in 2005, China grew 182mt, India 137mt, Indonesia 54mt, Bangladesh 40mt and Burma 25mt. Rice used to be cultivated in the Carolinas using slave labour until emancipation, but it then became uneconomical and it is now grown with very sophisticated tilling and water management in California.

Almost all of it is consumed by humans as brown rice, the most nutritious state before the husk is removed. White rice used in the West is milled, which removes much of the goodness before polishing and, in some cases, some of the nutrients being replaced.

Although rice can be grown on the uplands, the majority of the crop is cultivated on submerged land in the coastal plains, tidal deltas and river basins, requiring a plentiful supply of water (6,000 tons of rainwater for 1 ton of harvested rice). The world crop benefited greatly from the Green Revolution in producing hybrids, and the global output rose steadily until the end of the last century when global stocks, that peaked at 150 million tons in 2001, declined by nearly a half. Production was adequate in 2007, but only India, Japan, Indonesia, Thailand and Burma might still be able to produce at previous rates with the onset of the climatic shifts described earlier.

Corn/maize and soybeans

Corn/maize, which was thought to have been first grown by the North American Indians, is a versatile plant that makes efficient use of water and nutrients. It is, however, sensitive to frosts which is why it is planted in the spring and yields poorly should there be excessive heat and drought at the time of silking.

Of the 692 million tons produced in 2005, the US grew 280mt, China 131mt, Brazil 35mt; Europe grows in excess of 25mt. With wheat and rice, the three crops occupy some 40% of the global arable area. From peak carry-over stocks of 200,000 tons in 1986, the global stocks had declined by half in 2004/5.

Around half of all corn used to be consumed as animal feed on the home farm, with added usage as the basis for bourbon, sweet corn, breakfast foods and so on. More recently, American farmers have been offered subsidies for the production of methanol, or wood alcohol, as a fuel additive, which has caused the tightness of supplies and price rises since 1993/4. Although methanol has been used in racing cars to reduce burning, it is being added to gasoline to reduce imports from sensitive areas. It is produced using methane, a component of natural gas. Another competitor for land are soybeans, increasingly in demand for animal feed in the US which is the major grower followed by Brazil and China.

Cotton

Cotton was first cultivated in India around 5000 BC from where it spread east to China and west to Egypt, Turkey and across the Atlantic to America. For many years it was the staple crop of the South where exports supported the Confederacy in foreign exchange until union blockades brought the trade to its knees. It is still vulnerable to the AMO (described in Chapter 1) where drought in the South East has reduced the US output by 31%. More recently, it is extensively grown in Texas, irrigated from the Ogallala Formation that, as the last chapter showed, is becoming stressed. Only producers in Turkey, India and South East Asia are likely to be able to maintain supply due to the increased tightness of suitable land.

By 2007, the largest cotton producers were: China, India, the US, Pakistan, Brazil, Uzbekistan and Turkey. Of these, Diapason reports that China's demand has risen rapidly since around 1998, outstripping the supply capacity that, to an extent, is being taken up by India, where national policy decrees that it should increase its global market share. Cotton is a very thirsty crop requiring a rainfall of between 24-48 inches, and sunlight for successful growth without irrigation. Already, US farmers are switching out of cotton to wheat and soybeans, with 2007 carry-over stocks being the lowest since 1994. This could become the dominant trend as diminishing arable land and rising food prices compete strongly for cotton growing areas.

References

- www.paztcn.wr.usgs.gov/rsch_highlight/articles/200404.html

- Diapason, World Trade Center, Avenue de Gratta-Paille 2 PO Box 476, CH-1000 Lausanne 30, Switzerland

- Food and Agriculture Organization of the United Nations www.fao.org

- *Browning Newsletter*, The Frazer Publishing Co. PO Box 494, Burlington, Vermont 05402 (November 2002)

- *China Watch Monthly* Reviewcom, February 2007

- *Climate and the Affairs of Men* by Dr I. Browning and Nels Winkless (Fraser, 1975)

- 'Comprehensive Assessment of Water Management in Agriculture, The' (IWMI PO Box 2075, Colombo, Sri Lanka)

- *Forces of Change*, The by H. Hobhouse (Sidgwick & Jackson, 1989)

- *Great Wave*, The by D. Hackett Fisher (OUP, 1996)

- *Guns, Germs and Steel* by J. Diamond (Jonathan Cape, 1997)

- *Little Ice Age*, The by B. Fagan (Basic Books, 2000)

- *Past and Future History* by Dr I. Browning and Dr E. Garriss (Fraser, 1981)

- *Riding the Business Cycle* by W. Houston (Little, Brown, 1995)

- *Water: The International Crisis* by R. Clarke (Earthscan, 1991)

- *Water Wars* by J. Bulloch and A. Darwish (Gollancz, 1993)

4

People and Climatic Shifts

Summary

During the 1920s and 1930s, Raymond H. Wheeler, Professor of Psychology at the University of Kansas, became interested in the relationship between human behaviour and climate. To accumulate evidence he mobilised a team of students who discovered many thousands of historical relationships that were then recorded in a 'Big Book'.

From this empirical research he deduced that there was a definitive pattern of events falling into a five hundred year cycle, suggesting that there is a regular shift of influence from East to West and back again. The last half-millennium was the turn of the West. Now the influence is turning East.

Probably even more important for the next twenty years was a one hundred year cycle of wet/dry and hot/cool combinations. From this, and the climatic shifts explained in Chapter 1, this chapter suggests that many sensitive parts of the world, in particular the Middle East and China, will suffer ongoing periods of unrest, surges of refugees and conflicts. Other continents, such as North America, will suffer markedly different climates from the present, which could detract from the authority of elected governments. These events will not be localised and could cause havoc in many parts of the world. They are considered in greater detail in the following chapters.

Introduction

The material in this chapter is taken largely from the work of Dr Wheeler who, with the deontological work of Dr Andrew Douglass and the climatic research of

Professor Ellsworth Huntington, assembled the available data on how climate has affected human culture back to the dawn of recorded history.

Douglass pioneered the dating of climatic events from tree rings. Working from the Lowell Observatory at Flagstaff, Arizona, he discovered the probability that the width of tree rings were an indication of the growth of plants and consequently climate: narrow rings were from undue dryness and wider rings abundant moisture. To confirm this he started with nearby pines to find matching records; he then went on to study the great Sequoias that date back to around 3,500 BC. His work was greatly assisted by tree-ring relationships from the wooded beams of ancient Aztec ruins; not only did the rings yield weather patterns, they also showed the strength of carbon dioxide, which gave him an indication of solar output.

Dr Huntington of Yale studied the relationships between human behaviour and climate early in the twentieth century. He took rainfall and temperature patterns over many centuries, as described in *Climate, the Key to Understanding Business Cycles* (see References). From this he derived two major cycles:

1. A **five hundred year** rhythm of major discontinuities, and

2. A **one hundred year** cycle where there are repeats of wet/dry and hot/cool synchronicities.

Five Hundred Year Cycle

The **Five Hundred Year Cycle** was explored in *Future Storm* as part of a technological cycle that ushered in the industrial revolution and now the information age. This rhythm goes back much further in time, which may help us to understand what could be social and political patterns for the twenty-first century. This shows in Diagram 6 that, for the last two and a half thousand years, cultural and political power moved from East to West and back again. This is a summary of Wheeler's work where the evidence mostly, but not always, follows his contention.

Diagram 6. Wheeler's Five Hundred Year Cycle

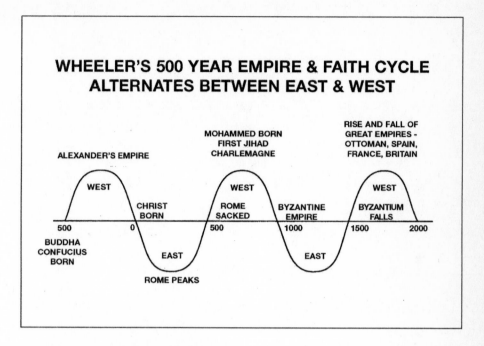

Source: www.cyclesresearchinstitute.org

Five hundred years to the birth of Christ

Five hundred years to the birth of Christ saw the flowering of the Greek Civilisation that spread around the Mediterranean and, in due course, passed its domination to Rome. The half-millennium also started with the birth of two men of wisdom: Buddha and Confucius – both of whom had a remarkable impact on the civilisation of the East. The former was an Indian prince who gave up everything to produce a gentle contemplative way of life where there was scope for the perfection of everyone through a number of incarnations. Confucianism, by contrast, suggested a worldly wisdom of duties, responsibilities and aspirations that gave China, in particular, a great sense of continuity and respect. In later years, the Roman Empire spread around the Mediterranean and north into France and Britain.

The first Five Hundred Years of the Christian Era

The first Five Hundred Years of the Christian Era began with the birth of the most remarkable man who ever lived. Although his ministry lasted for only three years, his apostles spread the Word throughout the eastern Mediterranean and most importantly to Rome where, in due course, it became the official faith of the empire. It could be said that while this period was not that of Eastern domination, those from the East destroyed the Roman Empire (described in Chapter 5).

Triggered by the terrible climatic conditions described in Chapter 1, the Hun hoards drove West to precipitate a cascade of fleeing people who oversaw the decline and fall of the Roman Empire that, by then, had divided into two with the East residing in Byzantium (later called Constantinople).

The Second Five Hundred Years of the Christian Era 501-1000 AD

The Second Five Hundred Years of the Christian Era, 501-1000 AD, is difficult to square with Wheeler's Western domination unless the First Jihad of the Muslim Era is taken as part of the West. While most of the West was sustained by the Roman church in the Dark Ages, the followers of the Prophet Mohammed swept through previously Christian Egypt, the eastern Mediterranean and into Turkey.

In the West, the Arab warriors moved along the North African coast, conquered Spain and were only defeated by Charles Martel at the Battle of Tours in 732, a hundred years after Mohammed's death. In Baghdad and in Córdoba on the Guadalajara there rose major civilisations that eclipsed anywhere in the Western Hemisphere. In the East, while India was still divided, China was starting to recover from a period of division.

The Third Half-Millennium of the Christian Era 1001-1500 AD

The Christian Era, from 1001 to 1500 AD, saw the consolidation of the nation state. After England was first united in 927 by Athelstan, it was over a hundred years later that the Eastern Church based in Constantinople separated from Rome and found adherents in the Balkans and in Russia. France only became united after the Hundred Years War in the fifteenth century, after a number of reverses when English kings, through the skill of their archers, controlled more of France than the monarch in Paris. Spain became an entity in 1492 when Ferdinand and Isabella defeated the Moors.

The early thirteenth century was a period of benign weather when many of the great cathedrals were built on both sides of the Channel. This changed in 1317/18, when famine swept western Europe; thirty years later most countries were again blighted by the Black Death that had hit parts of Europe 800 years earlier. Together with the Hundred Years War, this created a great loss of life. But there were compensations.

In England, the Black Death heralded the end of serfdom; but perhaps the greatest benefit to mankind was the Italian Renaissance. Those who escaped the horrors of the 'great dying' created a tremendous period of the arts, painting, architecture, learning and science. It is difficult to see how Wheeler identified this half millennium as being the turn of Eastern domination unless one takes into account one of the foremost military commanders of all time.

Genghis Khan, like Attila the Hun, came from a Mongolian tribe with a genius for military leadership. In a short space of time he had overturned the Ch'in Dynasty, leaving devastation wherever he went. China was divided north and south with the Great Khan's grandson, Kubla, dominating the north. Perhaps Wheeler was thinking of the Ming fleet of 3,000 vessels that in 1421 was reputed to have conquered the Indian Ocean, then circled the world.

The Fourth Half-Millennium of the Christian Era 1501-2000

This was certainly the turn of the West. By 1500 the technology that was to drive the Industrial Revolution was known but not exploited until some 200 years later. It made those countries able to develop it rich, powerful and ambitious. From the first Western voyage of Christopher Columbus across the Atlantic, seafarers explored the Americas and to the East, India, South East Asia, China and later Africa – each country imposing its own system of colonisation.

Nearer home it led to the development of great and powerful countries such as Germany, France, Britain and latterly the United States, which all gained supremacy through trade and numerous wars. In the twentieth century this led to two World Wars, after which military, industrial, financial and technical power went across the Atlantic to America. To the East there was a reversal of colonisation largely driven by the failure of the West as countries sought to govern themselves.

This movement was led by the Indian subcontinent, then to others including Indonesia, China, and Malaysia. The independence of Africa came later, with less beneficial results for its inhabitants. As the old millennium ended and the new one beckoned, the East was becoming resurgent once again in some directions, just as Wheeler predicted. But the twentieth century left unfinished business that those in the future will have to address and overcome.

The Third Millennium in the Christian Era

The Third Millennium in the Christian Era is already showing some of the throwbacks from the previous five hundred years (1500-2000). Consider the parallels:

• The printing press had been invented in 1453. That produced more books than ever before and was even starting to communicate news.

• The first stage of globalisation had been taken eight years earlier.

• Europe was trembling from the onslaught of the Second Jihad of the Ottoman Turks, who were halfway up the Balkans having already taken Constantinople in 1453.

• There was raging inflation from Spanish gold chasing too few providers of goods.

- The weather was terrible, causing England alone to have three periods of famine during the century.

- The greatest power on earth, the Catholic Church and the Holy Roman Empire, was about to be shaken by an Augustinian monk, who, objecting to its venality, declared independence from Rome.

- Europe's population was just recovering from the ravages of the Black Death.

- The technology that drove the Industrial Revolution was known.

Not all these factors are paralleled today, but enough to make us pause and reflect on the legacy of the previous century.

- The **oceanic oscillations** described in Chapter 1 will make life uncomfortable for over 20 years into the new century. As previous chapters have shown, it is likely that those who had excess water will have enough, while those which had only enough will suffer drought.

- The **refugee problem** described in Chapter 5 will become much more pronounced and will bring concerns over disease.

- **Global arable land** is being seriously depleted through salinity, thinning topsoil and increasing desertification; a third will be out of action by 2020. Many of these problems will be present in China, Central Asia and points west to the Middle East. Although east India will be well watered by the monsoon, the rest of the country is already stressed to feed its bourgeoning population.

- The **water supply** in many parts of the developing world has become contaminated and many people are dying. This is a problem that can cause mass movements and conflicts over water.

- The **world's financial system** has become greatly overstretched and in 2008 is showing definite signs of fracturing in some credit markets. If this is not addressed, governments who believe in state omnipotence will be unable to manage many of their present functions that are often indifferently run.

- Perhaps the **unusual individual** that Wheeler saw was needed to solve these fearful problems will arise to save the world from itself.

All these events could serve to herald the Information Age and the turmoil in society that it is likely to cause. But there are exciting nuggets of things to come. The darkness of the 1930s was a period of great innovation that flowered after the War. This is a summary of innovations to be described in Chapter 8 and the years to come that will make a major contribution to the next golden age.

- **Solar power**, even in temperate zones, could become a highly economical source of domestic and commercial energy.

- The **fuel cell** has the potential for generating compact power and will encourage hydrogen as the new fuel.

- **Cold fusion**, the ability to create energy from uniting deuteron (also known as heavy water, an isotope of hydrogen) into helium has the capacity to relieve the global water shortage through desalination plants.

- There is the prospect of producing **food needing less water**.

- Progress in **communications** will enable even greater independence for the individual who will be affected by Wheeler's work in a different way.

Hundred Year Cycle

Wheeler's Hundred Year Cycle was probably his core work, where he synthesised his analysis on human behaviour with his observation of climatic cycles over a hundred year period. He was the first to acknowledge that the length of his cycle could be from 70 to 120 years, but he first had to relate this to human behaviour. The general shape of his work with alternating phases of hot/cool and wet/dry is shown in Diagram 7.

Before analysing this in more detail, Wheeler had some suggestions on how we behave in hot or cool atmospheres. He explained that only a third of all muscular activity goes in physical work, with much of the rest going in heat generation.

When the ambient temperature is hot the sweat glands are not able to discharge at a high enough rate and the effort has to be reduced. The converse happens when it is cooler: the glands work efficiently and the body can continue to work while getting rid of the heat.

It is held that this also applies to mental activity. In a hot climate people feel lethargic and, through no fault of their own, their metabolic processes slow down, as does the heart and breathing; appetite lessens. This view was established long before the general introduction of air conditioning, which creates a better working environment, but his work has general applicability.

A leading anthropologist, Professor Ellsworth Huntingdon, held that the ideal temperature for mental performance was 38 degrees F and between 48-70 degrees F for physical action. This is found in a belt that in the Northern Hemisphere stretches from Great Britain, across northern Europe to the Black Sea and the Ural Mountains; it includes central China, North America and Japan. In the south the equivalent latitude includes South East Australia, New Zealand, and parts of South America.

This contention has been confirmed through a controlled experiment with rats at the University of Kansas. The rodents were divided into three groups, put into cool, ambient and warm environments and allowed to acclimatise for 40 days. These were the results:

- Those in the cool group (at 55 degrees F) were able to solve a food-maze puzzle in an average of 21 attempts. They were more alert, were not aggressive, had big litters, brought up their young with care, and the next generation were every bit as alert as their parents.

- By contrast, those in the warm group (kept at 90 degrees F) took an average of 56 tries to solve the food puzzle. They were less sexually motivated, had smaller litters and were careless bringing up their young (eating or maiming some of them). The next generation were even more listless, irritable and bad tempered.

- The control group were held at the ambient temperature and did not behave as the cool group, but better than those at 90 degrees.

It is of interest that the same group of rats, when swapped around to more stimulating or enervating environments, behaved in the same way as those in the former experiment. People from a temperate climate before air conditioning, however, had the capacity to adapt themselves to a warmer climate by changing their working hours to the early morning or evening when their energy levels were similar to those at home. Wheeler identified a cycle of four phases, shown in the following diagram.

Diagram 7. Raymond Wheeler's basic 100-year Climatic Cycle showing the phases over a cycle

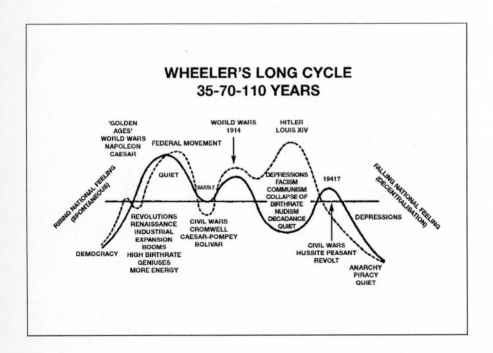

Source: www.cyclesresearchinstitute.org

Cold/dry phase

The cold/dry phase is the period of maximum energy where food can be short and the lack of a normal diet makes us aggressive and individualistic. This is a period of civil wars, emancipation, weak governments, migrations, class struggles and major reforms; over 90% of all who became known as great men come from such times. This is the phase of large families and simple lifestyles when art, architecture and ornamentation become functional and realistic, not unlike the work of the great Dutch painters of the seventeenth century. It is the time for a return to basic faiths when fads are not tolerated.

A typical equivalent period is the seventeenth century. Then there were civil wars, reforms, strongly held religious views, famines and migrations around the Northern Hemisphere in latitudes from 40 to 50 degrees north in England, Germany, Turkey, Holland, China, Japan and in the nascent Puritan colony in New England.

Referring to the diagram, there is a short period of warm/dry before the energy in the first period erupts into the second phase.

Warm/wet phase

The warm/wet phase arises from the austerity of the previous period as the sunspot cycle becomes positive. The early part of this 'spring' is when energy flows into optimism, a rising birth rate, high mental and physical activity, achievement and expansion. This is what Wheeler described as the Golden Age, when enlightened governments reign over great achievements and 90% of the rulers described as 'good' managed in these periods. This is an era of optimism, building, creativity and plenty, as crops grow in the abundant rainfall.

All this encourages a flowering of the arts, literature, music, scientific achievements, revivals of learning and economic expansion. As the phase continues, it often mutates into wars of expansion when the flourishing economy and people's exuberance flows over into aggression in the belief that other countries can be managed and developed to greater advantage for the attacker.

Typical periods of history may be the early part of the thirteenth century, when great cathedrals with spires 'reaching the heavens' were built. Others may be the Italian Renaissance, Elizabethan England and the Industrial Revolution. Much later, in the early part of the twentieth century, the presidency of Theodore Roosevelt led Americans to believe that anything seemed possible.

This cannot last for long for very soon enlightenment becomes bureaucratic and what was benign becomes authoritative in the next phase.

Warm/dry phase

The warm/dry phase is probably the most dangerous as the hot, dry climate produces food shortages, when lethargic and submissive people are prepared to obey powerful rulers and dictators. This is a period of moral, family and economic decline; also the birth rate falls to the chagrin of the dictators who want more soldiers to fight their wars. One can expect rising nationalism, fanaticism and the intolerance that are all parts of a police state.

The exuberance and elegance of the previous artistic period gives rise to rounded structures such as mosques with curved arches and windows typical of the Norman period; artists like Dali and Picasso produce surrealistic and imaginative work. In public life, the banners, power symbols, serried ranks of helmeted men and explosive speeches so blatantly displayed at the Nuremberg Rally, are manifestations of the 'master race'.

The 1930s were typical of this period for many countries, associated with pogroms, concentration camps, state media, a police state and wars.

Tyrants die or are assassinated, people tire of overt aggression and count the cost of conflict. This gives way to an easier period.

Cool/wet phase

The cool/wet phase heralds a return to prosperity, increased investment and more active global trade with the crops starting to grow in abundance and the cool climate creating more vigour. Wheeler observed that this period enables people to express their feelings in literature, music becomes more lyrical and art becomes more representational. He argued that this period also generates great religious leaders such as Confucius and Jesus Christ.

As individuals demand more freedom, there is a revival of national spirit and dominating governments become intolerable. People experience increased mental vigour, their health improves and the economy revives. The vigour extends to overseas expansion and colonisation – trade, particularly in agriculture, revives.

Typical periods in history were the wars of independence in Latin America and could have been the trigger for the rebellions in several European capitals in 1848.

Applications to the present

Referring back to Chapter 1, it is unlikely that the globe will experience the same climate all over unless there is a period of excessively high or low sunspots, or there is a very large volcanic eruption. However, we can apply Wheeler's reasoning to different areas of the world. Now, when the ocean oscillations are in the most difficult phase, we can expect unusually powerful contrasts, probably until the middle of the third decade of the twenty-first century. This also has considerable application to the following chapters.

- The **cool/dry** areas caused by a cooler northern Pacific will affect north China, Central Asia and north-east Asia. This could be extended to much of central and eastern Russia and central North America if there were major volcanic action. By the previous analysis, these areas will be ripe for individual aggression, civil wars, migrations and the overturn of dictatorships.

- **Warm/wet** places will be in two significant areas: the first, around both sides of the North Atlantic in the higher latitudes and in South East Asia. The second group will incorporate southern China, South East Asia and much of the eastern India subcontinent, which should have abundant rainfall.

- **Warm/dry** areas represent some of the most dangerous places on earth to spawn dictatorships. They are likely to include countries around the Mediterranean, much of the Middle East, Afghanistan, Pakistan and East Africa. Many of the southern European countries experienced dictatorships during the 1930s and this could happen again but would probably not be catastrophic for world peace. However, should hard men come to power around the Middle East, limiting the supply of oil, the Mediterranean could become very dangerous. The conditions in the southern states of the USA could replicate movements similar to the socialist-style of Huey Long when governor of Louisiana in the 1930s.

- **Cool/wet** climates could be the experience of the north-west coast of North America so distancing it from centres of government in Washington DC and Ottawa.

References

- *Climate, the Key to Understand Business Cycles*, by Raymond H.Wheeler & Zahorchak (editor) (Tide Press, 1983)

- *Riding the Business Cycle,* by William Houston (Little Brown 1995)

- *Booms, Depressions and Tree Rings,* by Raymond H. Wheeler (Weather Science Foundation, 1952)

- Raymond H Wheeler, Cycles Research Institute (www.cyclesresearchinstitute.org)

- Writings of Raymond H. Wheeler Foundation for the Study of Cycles

5

The Coming Wave of Refugees

Summary

The climatic changes described earlier and potential conflicts described in later chapters are very likely to create a huge refugee problem in the early decades of the twenty-first century. This is on very few agendas, but history tells us that unless we are aware of the difficulties and make some preparations, it will create huge disruptions for the developed world.

This chapter first examines the history of how refugees are caused, their reasons, and the advantages or disadvantages for their host nation. We then suggest how to cater for their mass movements and the diseases they are likely to carry with them in an attempt to prevent millions dying or nations dislocated.

Introduction

The United Nations agency UNHCR (United Nations High Commissioner for Refugees) reports that by June 2007 there were about ten million refugees in the world and roughly the same number of displaced persons; these were divided between one third from Asia and around a quarter from Africa. The work of the commission is mandated to lead and co-ordinate international action protecting refugees, resolve refugee problems and safeguarding their rights and well-being. The remit, according the 1951 Convention of the Status of Refugees, establishes its legal framework.

To understand more about how refugees are caused we need to examine how people have been displaced in the past in three primary ways, through:

1.   political spite

2.   famine and mass migrations, and for

3.   economic betterment.

Political spite

Political spite has been a dominant factor in causing human misery, so we can start to identify the turning points that made once valued citizens into apparent pariahs in the last five hundred years.

The unification of Spain under Ferdinand and Isabella led to the evacuation of non-Catholics. There was then the persecution of the Huguenots in France and later by Louis XIV. Finally, there was the rolling persecution of the Jews through the Russian pogroms and the horrors of the Holocaust.

Spain

One of the first deliberate acts of forced evacuation was after the defeat by Ferdinand and Isabella of the Moors from their Grenada stronghold in 1492, so ending an occupation of nearly 800 years. The invasion that started back in 711 was part of the remarkable First Jihad initiated after the Prophet's death (and is described in *Future Storm*, see References). The Moors converted the largely Vandal population to Islam and made their capital, Córdoba, one of the greatest seats of learning in Europe.

Although a small Christian enclave remained in Asturias and in present-day Portugal, it took 200 years before any determined action was made to regain the northern provinces, and another 200 years before central Castille was taken. Three more centuries elapsed before the Moorish stronghold of Grenada was captured under the joint authority of the two monarchs, Ferdinand and Isabella. Before this, the fanatical Benedictine monk Tomás de Torquemada – himself a converted Jew – had applied to the Pope to allow an inquisition that was granted in 1478. The main purpose of this was to root out heresy – particularly among the 100,000 Jews who had accepted baptism. Many were suspected of covertly carrying on their old faith, and so were practising heresy. This was not the only reason. There were many in the upper classes who owed money to the Jews and would have been happy to see their creditors fail.

By 1492, Torquemada persuaded the rulers to expel 160,000 Jews who had not converted, to be followed ten years later by a similar number of Muslims. Those suspected of heresy were tried and, if found guilty, perished in auto-da-fé, a staged ceremony like the show trials enacted by Hitler and Stalin. The inquisition continued in Spain until 1834. It seems incredible to us today that the Spanish authorities either murdered or expelled the Moors who understood farming, and the Jews who understood commerce and banking, but this stupidity was apparently not learned by later generations.

Spain again created thousands of refugees during and after the Spanish Civil War (1936-9). It was a conflict where more died from reprisals from both sides than from the actual combat. As General Franco's Nationalist forces advanced towards the Socialist stronghold in Catalonia, thousands of refugees swarmed across the French border where they were put into camps while the French authorities decided what to do with them. Among the choices open were to help with the construction of the Maginot Line or joining the anti-fascist forces where they fought bravely for the Allies.

The Spanish were not the only Latin race to forget history.

France

French Catholics had their own problems later in the sixteenth century when many people were converted to the new Protestant contagion. Spreading from Germany, and unfettered by having to observe many saints days, they became prosperous and were soon persecuted, with many fleeing to the free city of Strasbourg and to Geneva where John Calvin dominated the city's spiritual life.

Two factions now emerged: the Protestants led by Admiral Gaspard II of Coligny and the Catholics led by the House of Guise and supported by the king's mother, Catherine de Medici. Seizing the opportunity, 3,000 of the leading Huguenots were brutally murdered by the Catholic factions on St. Bartholomew's Day while attending a wedding in Paris on August 23rd 1572. The massacre was welcomed by Philip II of Spain and the Pope had a medal struck to honour the event. There followed other Protestant pogroms in provincial cities.

Most of the surviving Protestants refused to accept Catholicism and took up armed conflict to defend themselves, with the stand-off continuing until the Edict of Nantes in April 1598 which allowed them to practice their faith. The truce continued until the reign of Louis XIV who revoked the Edict, causing an estimated 400,000 to flee to England, Prussia, Holland and America. There, they became model citizens whose skills and energy greatly helped England in particular to start the Industrial Revolution. Their absence from France held back their country of origin in the Napoleonic Wars.

Russia

Russia had established what became known as the Pale of Settlement in the early years of the nineteenth century to establish areas where Jews, driven from the partition of Poland, were allowed to settle, including areas around the Black Sea annexed from Turkey. Later, Jews came under increased restrictions in Poland, Lithuania, Belarus, the Ukraine and so on.

Although there had been anti-Jewish movements in many parts of the world, the worst pogroms, as they became known, started in 1881 when some blamed the Jews for the murder of Tsar Alexander II. This was probably a pretext because, as in Spain, the Jews were more industrious and smarter than the locals, which caused considerable resentment. A number of homes and businesses were attacked and burnt with the tacit support of the police and authorities. Many were killed.

There were more bloody massacres in 1903 to 1906 when many Jews, among others, were killed. Both these movements fuelled the mass exodus of Jewish people, who settled primarily in America but also in Britain. Their contribution to their new countries in banking, publishing, the media, the retail trade and many other areas was of great benefit to their hosts and a huge loss to their persecutors.

In late nineteenth century Russia, the serfs had been liberated from their bondage in 1861 when many in the Ukraine had bought their own land and prospered. Despite their good contribution to harvests, private enterprise ran counter to the communist collectivisation of agriculture. While it was voluntary to join the collective in other states, it was made compulsory in the Ukraine in the early 1930s, when Stalin sent enforcers under Molotov to confiscate all grain, beet, potatoes, vegetables and any other food to ensure compliance. It was called the *Holodomer* and destroyed around 1.5 million people, with another 300,000 being forcibly resettled to work in the Urals and Central Asia. Predictably farmers destroyed grain rather than give it voluntarily and, with this coming at a time of harsh weather, the harvest failed; apart from those forcibly deported, people were disallowed from migrating, so adding to the misery. The action succeeded in ensuring the Wehrmacht would be welcome in the Ukraine. It was also responsible for eliminating anyone who knew how to manage their own farm – just like the actions of Ferdinand and Isabella nine centuries earlier with the Moors.

Germany

Germany was responsible for by far the worst pogrom with the Holocaust, although it is not known whether Hitler was influenced by events in Russia; more likely it was his pre-First World War experience in Vienna where he lived as a vagabond. However, the Führer was not the only German disliking Jewry for their prominent position in banking, commerce and retailing – although they had fought bravely for the Kaiser in the First World War.

The Nazi pogroms were more calculated than those of the Russians and could have alerted potential migrants of the horrors to come. First to be passed were the Nuremberg Laws restricting Jewish activity, followed by a progressive squeeze culminating in November 1938 when shops and synagogues were fired in, which became known as Kristallnacht. This wonton act by the SA drove over 100,000 to flee Germany to enrich Britain and America once again. For those remaining, apart from the German death camps, many countries such as Poland and Rumania conducted their own pogroms, probably for the same jealous and arrogant reasons as the Nazis.

Uganda

Uganda's president, Idi Amin, in an act of economic insanity expelled around 80,000 Asians in November 1972. These people, who had contributed largely to the wealth of the country in industry, commerce and the professions, were given three months to depart leaving their possessions behind. They moved primarily to Britain but also to Canada and the United States, where most became model citizens contributing greatly to their new country.

In almost every case cited above the evicting country was the loser. Those made refugees mostly became valuable and able citizens in their host countries.

Famine

Throughout history famine has been a major cause of exodus – whether it was in Europe in 1317-18, famines during the Maunder Minimum during the seventeenth century, or the terrible Chinese famine in 1958-61 under Mao. All these movements were people fleeing in search of food.

Famine, then, is mostly associated with subsistence agriculture, where large numbers of people suffer when resources, primarily water, fall below the ability of the land to carry them. These conditions have not been helped by the conditions described in Chapter 3 with land that has been overworked, deforested and eroded. Another is the inability of people to acquire essential food, such as the Irish Potato Famine.

Famine destroys livelihoods but does not force starvation immediately. First, people will attempt to cope by rationing consumption and trying to find alternative sources of income. Next, they will sell off plots of land to stay alive. Only finally will they either migrate or stay and starve. These are some examples of how famines are caused:

- The **Thirty Years War** (1618-48) caused the greatest number of deaths when religious factions fought over Germany. Around a third of the population perished when hungry soldiers took every bit of food from a population already near starvation. More recently, war has been the cause of starvation in Africa when millions have died as one tribe seeks to gain ascendance (or control of resources such as oil or minerals) over another group. The famine in Darfur seems a deliberate act of the Sudanese government to eliminate a number of their own people.

- Climatic shifts have been responsible for many disasters such as the **seven abundant and seven lean years** described in Genesis, the Torah and the Koran. The Nile occupies only a small area of Egypt but supports the population when the river floods to a satisfactory level to deposit the loess and water the soil; unless Egypt can import food, the failure of the Nile will cause starvation as it did in the seven bad years.

- **Potato disease in Ireland** led to the famine of 1845-49 that destroyed many lives and forced millions to migrate to America. The Irish had no law of primogenitor, which obliged the land to be divided between the sons who each had a progressively smaller holding. A farmer could support his family by growing potatoes in a lazybed, a long furrow. When the fungus *Phytophthora infestans* struck, it rotted potato fields overnight. The peasants' plight was made desperate when the authorities continued the free market in food that was actually sold to England at higher prices than the Irish could afford.

- The greatest number of deaths occurred in **China in 1959-61** when some thirty million died when Mao continued to insist that food be sold abroad to pay for his mania to industrialise.

Mass migrations

Mass migrations have been the stuff of speculation and fear throughout the ages. Who were these people who made such a perilous mass exodus from their traditional areas to terrorise lands and people that had grown prosperous in the West and in China? Dr Iben Browning, an historical climatologist, was in no doubt and cited an 800-year cycle of drought in central Asia that had propelled people to find new homes. He cited a movement around 1200 BC that brought the plague to Egypt and 800 years later, at the time of the Peloponnesian War with Sparta, Athens had a serious bout of the bubonic plague that so seriously weakened the city that it lost the war. These early migrations are not well documented, the next two are.

Attila the Hun

Attila the Hun was the most powerful of a line of Hunnish kings who came from Mongolia at the end of the fourth century, at a time of famine when many were moving from north to southern China to escape destruction. After an unsuccessful foray into China, the tribes of mounted warriors armed with powerful bone bows moved west. Attila, born in 406, did not succeed until 432, after the Huns had settled in Hungary driving out the Ostrogoths and Visigoths – who were themselves attacking the Roman Empire – forcing them to move south towards the Balkans. Alaric was a Visigoth who sacked Rome in 410.

The other group to flee the Huns were the Vandals, a Germanic people, who moved west through Gaul then south through Spain and North Africa where they settled. Attila also drove west into France leaving destruction in his wake, but was defeated in 451. He then moved south into Italy and died in 453.

The immense power of these warriors created a huge refugee problem for Europe that destroyed the Roman Empire. Apart from the Goths and Vandals, England, the northernmost outpost of the Roman Empire, was invaded by the Angles and Saxons from the east and the Picts from the north. The Huns not only brought destruction, they also carried the bubonic plague into the West where it devastated many countries, including Constantinople that did not fall to the invaders but suffered terribly. Amongst the carnage, one group of people benefited. Some Italian merchants, fearful for their trade and safety, settled on some mud flats in a lagoon in the north-east of the peninsula thus creating the city of Venice.

Eight hundred years later the greatest warrior chief of all time brought destruction and the plague to China and Europe.

Genghis Khan

Genghis Khan was born around 1167. Son of a warrior chief, by the age of 39 he had succeeded in uniting all the Mongol tribes. Stimulated by extreme climatic conditions, he moved south-east to invade China and destroyed the Chin Empire capturing Beijing in 1215; his grandson Kubla went on to rule northern China. The Great Khan then turned his attention to the Muslim states in Central Asia, operating with the simple strategy of demanding surrender and a large payment or later destruction. He never lost an engagement. As he moved west he collected a number of Turkic warriors who soon outnumbered the Mongols. By 1227 he reached the Caucasus where he died, having divided his empire among his sons.

The Mongol Empire stretched at one time from the Mediterranean to Korea through the exploits of Khan's successors, who in a brilliant campaign moved up the frozen rivers to annihilate southern Russia and destroy Kiev; they then turned west and defeated a Polish/German army at Legnica. It was held that Christian Europe was only saved from destruction by the death of Khan Ogedei. The only reverse suffered by the Mongol army was their defeat by the Egyptian Mamelukes at Nazareth in 1260. The Mongol Empire ended with the death of Tamerlane in 1405, but his influence helped to trigger the greatest Islamic empire of the Ottoman Turks that endured for nearly 600 years.

We now await the next 800 year invasion. This time will it be the bubonic plague?

Economic migration

Economic migration was prevalent in the latter part of the twentieth century when individuals from previously colonial territories moved primarily into Europe to better their condition. However, unlike the Jews or Huguenots, most did not carry their skills with them; in most countries they were welcome as they performed tasks others found distasteful, and governments in a sense of misplaced benevolence paid their own citizens to remain idle. Economic migration has been endemic in recent years from EU enlargement. Under the freedom of movement laws, people from Eastern Europe have moved west, many carrying skills and a work ethic. However, less welcome have been others with fraudulent or criminal habits learned under a communist regime.

Displacement diseases

Apart from the plague carried by the Huns and Mongols, possibly the most notorious were the viruses of measles and smallpox carried by the Spanish Conquistadors to the New World – these wiped out more Aztecs and Incas than ever fell in combat. It is argued that the defeated nations got their own back by giving syphilis to the returning Spaniards, which wiped out many of the Iberian upper classes. More recently, mutations of sexually transmitted and other diseases have been discovered that are defying classic treatments. First among these must be the greatest killer of the developing world – tuberculosis.

Tuberculosis

Tuberculosis (TB) is a disease that primarily attacks the lungs of people living in unsanitary conditions. It reached near epidemic proportions in the rapidly growing industrialised societies in Europe and North America during the eighteenth and nineteenth centuries. Only in the early twentieth century did improved hygiene and health reduce the number of fatalities.

Mycobacterium tuberculosis is a rod-shaped bacterium that spreads through coughing, sneezing or even when talking, and attacks the lungs to form a lesion which, unless treated, spreads into the bloodstream and through the body. Its symptoms are lack of energy, weight loss and persistent coughing. As the lesion spreads through the lungs, the patient dies from being unable to breathe from toxaemia and general exhaustion. Before antibiotics, patients were given long periods of rest and, if necessary, the surgical removal of the lesion. Now, being a bacteria, it can be treated with a range of drugs.

Typhus

Typhus has been one of the greatest human scourges in history. It is prevalent among people in the unsanitary conditions found in prisons, concentration camps and refugee ships; it will also be present in the large expanded cities that house nearly half the world's population. It was a scourge in the Thirty Years War in seventeenth century Germany, in the Napoleonic Wars and during famines, such as the Irish Potato disaster. More recently, prisoners in Korean camps died of typhus. It used to be called the 'soldiers disease' because it was responsible for often wiping out more combatants than fell in action.

It is carried by lice which, having caught the bacteria from a sufferer, move to another victim where it ejects infected excreta that then enters the wound when the itch is scratched; it is no consolation to the patient that the louse also dies. The symptoms are a sudden onset of fever with headaches, chills and general pains with a rash appearing around the third day. If not treated, death from toxaemia comes after two or three weeks. The best antidote is to kill the lice through pesticides and treat the individual through appropriate drugs such as chloramphenicol.

Waterborne diseases

Waterborne diseases, such as typhoid fever, could also be carried by refugees fleeing from overcrowded conditions with polluted water supplies. The *Salmonella typhi* bacteria enters the body through ingesting contaminated food or water, when it penetrates the intestinal wall and multiplies. The symptoms are similar to typhus and are accompanied by loss of appetite, and persistent diarrhoea or constipation. The patient may recover from their own immune system, otherwise death comes from peritonitis, heart failure, pneumonia or meningitis.

Cholera is a destructive bacterial infection caused by drinking polluted water that enters the small intestine to cause acute diarrhoea with rapid depletion of body fluids and essential salts; unless these are corrected, the bacteria causes acute dehydration and shock. Cures include replacing salts, fluids and antibiotics.

Smallpox could be used as a terrorist weapon which, in an age when it has nearly been eliminated, could be used to kill millions – the reason why President Bush has offered vaccination to US citizens. It is a highly contagious disease which, when contracted, has an incubated period of fourteen days before the victim contracts a fever then a heamhorragic rash that is often fatal. It was so lethal that armies in Napolionic times were often vaccinated.

Robin Clarke, in *Water: The International Crisis*, reports that **400 million people are suffering from gastroenteritis**, another 200 million from bilharzias (a disease attacking the bowels from contaminated water), a further 200 million from threadworms, 160 million from malaria and around 30 million from onchocerciasis, a disease caused bv the nematode worm.

AIDS

AIDS is the second biggest killer in the developing world, where the percentage of fatalities is estimated to rise from 8.5% of the total to over 37% by 2020. After being first identified in 1981 in Los Angeles, it spread rapidly among the homosexual and drug-taking communities, infecting around 750,000 in the US by the end of the decade. However, 90% of cases now occur in Africa, India and China where it is more often a heterosexual disease.

The AIDS virus is not contagious but is transmitted though exposure to infected blood, semen, excreta and through breast milk. The first stage is the human immunodeficiency virus (HIV) and the symptoms after a few weeks may include nausea, muscle soreness, fever, rash, sore throat, diarrhoea, and so on. Although these symptoms may disappear the immune system deteriorates to make the infected person more liable to catch such complaints as pneumonia, herpes, tuberculosis, tongue and rectal cancers; at the same time the body becomes progressively emaciated. Eventually, after ten years AIDS becomes full blown and the body ceases to have the ability to fight off anything malignant.

The target of the HI virus are the T4 helper cells, the principal immune system cells that stimulate others to resist disease. Viruses need a host cell to multiply and with HIV they enter through a protein. Once inside the virus then multiplies rapidly and goes through many mutations, making any antidotes very difficult to formulate, although inhibitors have been developed to slow the spread of the disease. The counters are mainly behavioural – practices that are difficult to change in some societies.

Bubonic plague

Finally, there is the scourge of the sixth and fourteenth centuries, the bubonic plague, that over the centuries has destroyed more lives proportionally than even the Spanish Flu of 1917-18. There is little record of those who died in Athens or of the plague carried by the Huns, but the Black Death of 1348-51 was responsible for the death of twenty-five million people in Europe. The bubonic plague came to Europe via a fort at Kafka in the Crimea peninsula besieged by the Mongols. The Genoese sailors prevailed against the attackers, but as a parting shot the Mongols catapulted in the torso of an infected prisoner. On their way home most of the Genoese died but the black rats, that are part of the disease cycle, carried the infection ashore to Italy.

It is not the rat bites that spread the plague but the infected fleas that hop onto humans in overcrowded and unsanitary conditions. It is no consolation to the victim that the rat and flea also die.

The other, and more deadly way of infection, is through aerosols – moisture carried by the breath in confined spaces. In both transmissions the bubonic bacteria

Yersinia pestis (y pestis) incubates for three to six days. After that, the patient complains of shivering, vomiting, headaches, giddiness, pains in the limbs and is feverish. As the temperature rises, painful buboes form in the groin and the armpits; the patient dies within three or four days. The plague can now be treated by antibiotics but most cases then were fatal.

Present attitudes to refugees

The Second World War displaced millions as the Wehrmacht slashed through Western then Eastern Europe and the Soviet Union. These were not just civilians; tens of thousands of combatants were removed and had to find their way home. Stalin despised those who had been taken prisoner and they often received a hostile reception on repatriation. One major incursion into the Middle East was the creation of the State of Israel in 1948, with all the disruption and future creativity that this involved.

The 1951 Convention on Refugees was formed by order of the United Nations and based in Geneva. Its remit is a curiously bland document which sets out how legal refugees should be treated in their host country: their right to earn a living, collect assets, travel and so on. It also stipulates that they should not forcibly be repatriated to countries where they would receive a hostile reception. There were some later amendments but none that are likely to meet the several conditions described in this chapter and elsewhere.

Curiously, the Convention does not refer to the plight of previous refugees as summarised earlier, nor the problems of disease. This might have been understandable after WWII, but scant attention was paid to the historical background in a UN publication called *Refugees and Forced Displacement*, edited by Edward Newman and Joanne Van Selm (see References).

Taking all this into account with other chapters in this book, it is possible to come to some views on the scale of the refugee problem, the likely target areas and, based on history, what could be done.

An approach towards a solution

Any solution to the refugee problem for the West has to be viewed in the context of the present day (early 2008):

1. First, the US has been the locomotive of the global economy with the American consumer commanding some 20% of the global GDP. Should the present trend of credit tightening and the decline in the housing market continue then consumer spending is likely to lag and government revenue will decline. As this is likely to be felt in other countries, governments will be obliged to review their welfare spending commitments downwards, both to their own people and to refugees. This would make the receiving country a less attractive target for economic refugees.

2. Rising unemployment and the need to reduce welfare and other transfer payments will require work for any benefit paid. There will be growing resentment towards migrants. Already in Britain half the babies born in London were to foreign-born mothers; many other cities face the same dilution. This is not singular to Britain – France, Germany, Italy and Holland, among others, are facing the same dilemma.

3. Migrants will be expecting the same level of social security as the natural citizens, but straightened government finances will require these to be cut back, as they were in the 1970s. If the migrants also bring disease there will be added resentment as the newcomers receive treatment that has been paid for by residents.

4. Chapters Six and Seven provide a foretaste from where the refugees will come:

    •   Drought in eastern Africa and conflict in the Middle East will propel a rising tide of desperate people towards the Balkans and southern Europe.

- Adverse conditions in northern China will drive many migrants to the south and to countries in South East Asia, particularly to Indonesia.

- Historically, as we have seen, there has been mass migrations from Central Asia to the West, bringing with them diseases for which their hosts may have little immunity.

5. To be positive, many countries need an infusion of talent and brawn to counter their demographic decline – particularly Russia where the native population is falling with diminished life expectancy. Wise governments will set about defining the skills they need from donor countries and making these potential migrants into citizens.

Dealing with the refugee problem

As we have seen, many refugees have proved loyal and constructive citizens to their host country and a number will have entered legally. However, the potential scale of illegal entry resembles the disruption to Europe by the Huns of the fifth century, an event that would totally destabilise existing societies. Any solution must include helping people to find a refuge nearer to their home.

At the same time it is inconceivable that civilized countries could accept that millions should be allowed to die because developed counties have put up impenetrable barriers. The globalisation of images alone would demand a humanitarian response and we can learn from the past. The following ideas should be considered.

Create a Security and Conservation Agency

Create a Security and Conservation Agency (CSA), which has a history going back at least to the 1930s when President Roosevelt created the Civilian Conservation Corps (CCC). This comprised young men from homes with no employed breadwinner to form what became known as the Tree Army. The idea was to give the unemployed an open-air life doing worthwhile jobs such as planting trees, disaster relief, building levees to prevent flooding, creating sites of special interest and so on.

The concept is expanded in the CSA where there would be at least two levels: local and national/international. The first is putting the unemployed to work today among their communities in towns and the countryside clearing litter, recovering dilapidated inner-city sites, restoring woodland, helping old people and so on.

The second group would be trained to work on a national and international scale in restoring sites of exceptional attraction, canals, disaster relief, fighting major fires, planting woodland, flood relief and so on. They could also be deployed overseas in several programmes as part of an international effort. They could support the improved irrigation and land restoration plan suggested in Chapter 3.

Build camps

Build camps within territories suffering from internal refugee problems, such as those in Zimbabwe and Darfur. These would be created and manned by the CSA and, if necessary, be guarded by paramilitaries. The aim would be to create a safe enclave where people could be settled. In conjunction with other agencies, they could be trained along the same lines as the CSA to manage the areas themselves, cultivate the land, start small businesses and so on. Where agriculture has been run down, as in Zimbabwe, emergency supplies would need to be imported until the area was self-supporting.

Mass displacements should be accommodated by camps set up, if possible, near the territories they have left, for the numbers concerned could run into millions. Failure to do this would mean that the developed world would be swamped by unsettled people.

The displacements could be managed by host nations of similar ethnic backgrounds. For example, Turkey might agree to be the focus of international effort relating to the Turkic peoples of Central Asia. It is a country with more than adequate water and it would have the authority and the international support to set up whatever facilities were needed to contain the onrush. A similar plan might be considered in Eastern Europe for people displaced from the East.

Developed countries such as those in Western Europe are likely to repatriate surplus economic refugees due to local rising unemployment and increasing resistance to 'foreigners' taking jobs that should rightfully belong to the home citizens. This would effectively end the right of EU citizens to work in other countries of the Union. The US might have to take similar measures.

Dysfunctional countries such as Zimbabwe might be temporarily taken over by the international community to act as a home for displaced people in the region. The idea would be to create a safe enclave for the homeless until their home regimes were safe.

Repatriation

Repatriation is a continual theme for excess refugees and a number have been able to cite their human rights not to be repatriated. There are undoubtedly a number that might fall into this category, but overall there would appear to be three main classes:

1. Members of a country expelled because of treason to their home country and all rights of citizenship removed. Convicted terrorists would come into this class. Removing the rights to habeas corpus would come into this category.

2. Repatriation to their own country for those who left for economic reasons. Included in this would be EU citizens considered earlier.

3. Finally, there would be those whom the host country wished to expel but would be in danger should they return to their own country. One solution would be to deport these people to one of the camps described earlier.

Developed nations will be obliged to set up a screening system similar to that in Australia where all illegal migrants would be contained in a camp then checked for their ability to contribute to the host nation at various levels. Those unable to be absorbed could be either sent home or be trained as contributors to the CSA organisation in other countries. Failure to achieve this would seriously damage the likely overstretched morale of the inhabitants.

References

- *Atlas of World History* (Times Books)

- *Refugees and Forced Displacement,* Edited by Edward Newman and Joanne van Selm (United Nations University Press, 2003)

- *The Spanish Civil War*, by Hugh Thomas (Penguin Books, 1968)

- The 1951 Refugee Convention

- www.unhcr.org

6

Prospects for Conflicts over Water and the Basis for Peace in the Middle East

Summary

With all eyes focussed on solving the Iraqi internal problems, less attention is being paid to the underlying cause of water being the potential for conflict. This chapter analyses each of the major players in the region and suggests that the combination of Turkey's capacity to store water and Israel's ability to use it efficiently is probably the ultimate lever to secure peace in the region when water shortages are becoming more prevalent. The chapter ends with a review of several scenarios that could happen before a settlement is reached.

Introduction

There have been numerous wars fought over water or the lack of it. *Future Storm* identifies an 800 year cycle of drought in Central Asia that was responsible for the incursions of Attila and Genghis Khan into Europe and China. There were major movements around the mid seventeenth century when the extreme dry, cold weather inflamed wars in England and Germany, while a civil war in China ended the Ming Dynasty. There was also an uprising against the Tokugawa regime in Japan, and the nascent Cape Cod colony in the New World nearly ended. More recently, water was responsible for wars in the Middle East.

Some indications where the next conflicts could take place due to the adverse oscillations in the great oceans were shown in Chapter 1. Of the greatest significance is the broad band of drought stretching from northern China, west through Central Asia and then south-west through the Middle East – particularly through Iran and Mesopotamia (shown in Diagram 3). Of further concern are the fifty countries on four continents that share more than three-quarters of their land in international river basins – with thirteen of these shared by five basins. This chapter will consider the critical areas of the Nile, Mesopotamia, and the Jordan and Yarmuk rivers shared by Syria, Israel, Palestine and Jordan.

The needs of water

The needs of water have been set out in some detail in earlier chapters. In particular the problems for the Middle East are set out in an MEMRI report (see References) that quoted the work of an Egyptian researcher Dr Hamid Abd Al-Adhim. He stated the needs of water for the Arab countries were 189.7 billion cubic meters of water (BCM) in 2002, up nearly a quarter from 1990, and due to rise much further by 2025. Egypt alone needed 70.5bcm in 2002 – expected to rise over 45% by 2025, when a water surplus would turn to a deficit by 2025. Similar problems will be experienced in Iraq, Libya, Oman, Jordan and the UAE. Adhim complains that **88% of the water entering Arab lands is controlled from non-Arab sources**; Egypt's similar dependence is 90%, Syria's is 50%.

A World Bank report states that the Middle East is by far the driest region in the world with only 1,200 cubic metres of water per person per year compared to a global average of 7,000. Particularly hard hit is the Jordan basin whose population has risen six fold since the 1940s; it needs 15bcm annually and only receives 3.5.

These conditions have become more acute in this decade when rising unemployment and reduced rainfall is creating additional tensions to an already stressed region. Since agriculture demands 70% of all fresh water, it is necessary to evaluate where conflicts may break out over the capacity of countries to feed themselves. These include Egypt, Iran, Iraq, Israel, Syria and Turkey. The aim is to establish a Drought Rating for the six countries based on the population related to arable land, modified depending upon the efficiency of agriculture and liability for drought – as set out below, a more full description of the method is in Chapter 7.

Country	Land K.sq.Km	Arable %	Population Million	Pop/sq Km	Efficiency Basis A	Drought Basis B	Drought Rating
Egypt	1,001	2.92	80.3	2769	1	1	2769
Iraq	432	13.1	26.7	472	1/3	1	157
Iran	1650	9.78	68.9	427	1	1.3	555*
Israel	20.7	15.5	6.35	1984	1/8	1	248
Syria	184	24.8	18.9	420	1	1	420
Turkey	770	29.8	70.4	307	1/3	0.66	67

Basis A: efficiency rating – percentage of population in agriculture

Between 2-5% – Million population/sq km divided by   8
Between 5-15% – Million population/sq km divided by   3
Above 15% – Million population/sq km divided by   1

Basis B: drought rating:

Drought very likely – multiplier for million population/sq km   1.33
Drought likely – multiplier for million population/sq km   1
Drought unlikely – multiplier for million population/sq km   0.66

Material taken from CIA Factbook/geos

* Iran may be given a lower rating because of considerable damed reserves.

On the basis of the Drought Rating, Egypt is by far the most vulnerable, relying almost totally on the Nile with 90% of its water sourced outside its borders. Further north, Syria has a high drought rating amidst a fractious area, receiving 50% of its water from Turkey with whom there have been disputes over the flow and quality of Euphrates water. Although Iran has a high rating it has probably enough dammed water for its population to drink and sufficient petrodollars to buy food. The following is an assessment of the major players.

Egypt

Egypt's history goes back to 3200 BC when the country was unified under the first pharaoh. Through the flooding of the Nile, its people were able to expand and prosper; as the deserts on either side were impassable, it could only be attacked from the Mediterranean in the north and Nubia to the south. The only known invaders until 341 BC from the north were the Hyksos people who were duly driven out.

The rule by ethnic Egyptians ended with the invasion by Persia, then by Alexander and later Ptolemy, one of Alexander's generals. The dynasty was replaced in the seventh century by Arabs as part of the First Jihad. They ruled for six centuries before the Mamelukes took control, followed by the Turks in 1517. In more modern times, the 1869 completion of the Suez Canal led to a British mandate which used Egypt as a base to fight the Turks in 1914 and Rommel in 1942. Egypt received full independence after the Second World War.

The Nile is the longest river in the world, flowing 4,169 miles from Lake Victoria through Uganda and into Sudan where it meets the Blue Nile at Khartoum. Being shared by ten countries, Egypt's position was first established in 1929 when it was allocated 48 billion cubic metres (bcm) a year with Sudan receiving 4bcm – later Egypt's quota was increased to 55.5bcm. With the population of the ten countries estimated to double from 2000 to 2030, there is increasing pressure on resources.

Already, 88% of all water is used by agriculture to contribute only 14% of Egypt's GDP. This will oblige the country to use water more efficiently if they are to sustain a rising standard of living. The World Bank has taken the initiative to bring together all those using the Nile in an attempt to avoid conflicts. This is clearly a noble objective, but decreased rainfall in East Africa has reduced the level of Lake Victoria to the lowest for 80 years – although this may change with the increasing tropics described in Chapter 1. The only solution for Egypt is for each upstream country to be as water conscious as Israel. Unsurprisingly, **Egypt has said it will declare war on any country restricting its flow of water**.

Iran

Iran is particularly significant because it controls the northern side of the Straits of Hormuz, through which navigates around a third of the world's oil exports – particularly to Japan and China but also to Europe, the USA and Latin America. Through their utterances, Iran's leaders seem determined to undermine the US and its support of Israel – a country they wish to eliminate. There follows some background to a country that has remained relatively dormant for centuries.

Despite invasions, the frontiers of Iran (Persia until 1935) have remained relatively static back to the time of Xerxes, when it threatened Greece and was eventually destroyed by Alexander in the fourth century BC. From the sixth century BC it had espoused Zoroastrianism (the classic battle between good and evil) but this was largely overwhelmed by the rise of the Muslim Empire shortly after the Prophet's death in 632. The Persians took the Shi'a minority form of Islam founded by Mohammed's son-in-law Ali, that gave the priestly class not only the power to rule but also to interpret the Koran – something not permitted by the Sunni caliphs or Sultans.

By the early twentieth century the country had started to create a source of oil wealth through what became the Anglo Iranian Oil Company at Abadan. This enabled the new shah, Reza Shah Pahlavi, to start modernising the country from 1925. He was succeeded by his eldest son Mohammed Reza Shah Pahlavi before the Second World War. Wishing to diminish the influence of the Soviet Union in the north and Britain in the south, he flirted with Nazi Germany but was obliged to cede to the dominant powers.

After the War the Shah formed an alliance with America and with their help built up a formidable armed force. At the same time he became increasingly dictatorial as he set about modernising the country, including social reforms and the release of women from Islamic standards – something that alienated powerful clerics. By the time of the revolution in 1979, Iran had enjoyed fifteen years of rising prosperity, an increasingly wealthy and worldly professional middle class, and a considerable, but poorer, lower middle and underclass.

It was to these, and the more strictly religious in the country, that the Ayatollah Ruhollah Khomeini appealed from his exile in Paris. Through the clergy he urged the people to depose the Shah, reject his secular corruption, and return to Islamic purity. Against the odds he returned in triumph and, despite the supposed loyalty of the army to the Shah, his followers ruthlessly swept aside any opposition and set out to create a theocratic – and anti-Western – state.

Rejecting any form of democracy, the ruling clerical Ulema set up revolutionary courts to eliminate by execution those deemed responsible for implementing the Shah's more distasteful policies. More importantly, Khomeini created the Islamic Revolutionary Guards (IRG). Under the direct command of the ruling Guardians Council, this group was responsible for storming the American embassy, subjugating dissidents to the regime and for spearheading the re-armament programme. It is from the fanatical IRG that President Mahmoud Ahmadinejad emerged.

The drive to acquire weapons did not, however, start with Ahmadinejad. After the siege of the US Embassy, America refused to supply spares or to recondition any of the military material supplied under Pahlavi's rule. This wrong-footed the Iranians when Saddam Hussein invaded in September 1988, and the Ayatollahs were obliged to seek arms from Syria, China and North Korea.

Worried about a renewal of the war with Iraq, the Iranians set about acquiring missiles. The first of these was the Oghab, a short-range weapon with a 3kg warhead to strike at Iraqi border cities. Later, the Scud-C was developed that was able to deliver a warhead well into Turkey; this was followed by the acquisition of Shahab-4/5 that was capable of transporting a nuclear warhead to Israel.

Later, the Iranians acquired the rights to build the Silkworm anti-shipping missile that was similar to the Exocet (the French sea-skimming device) that could be launched either from shore batteries or from fast-attack boats. They called it the Tondar and it is thought a great number are deployed to cover the Straits of Hormuz. More recently, Russian Tor-M1 anti-missile missiles are being deployed around the sensitive nuclear sites.

As part of the drive to defend their borders, the urge to acquire nuclear weapons was initiated by Ali Akbar Hashemi Rafsanjani, the so-called moderate speaker of Majlis, the parliament, and sometime president of Iran. Initially there was an attempt to buy these illegally from Central Asia disassembled, but critical parts were found missing and this avenue was summarily aborted. However, during a mission to North Korea in 1993, Kim Il Sung agreed to make the technology of the Pakistani nuclear physicist Dr A. Q. Khan available to Iran.

The process of acquiring the highly specialised equipment for converting yellow-cake uranium oxide into weapon-grade uranium and plutonium is told in fascinating detail by Kenneth Timmerman in *Countdown to Crisis*. It required using Khan's subterfuge methods to get the machine tools, furnaces and instruments from the West and deploy these in sites near Tehran and Isfahan. At the latter there is a declared facility for producing uranium hexafluoride (UF_6) in centrifuges at an underground site to extract the fissile U235. When completed there is evidence that it could produce enough material for 20-30 nuclear devices per year.

Iran is mostly rugged and mountainous with less than 10% of its land arable; the climate is variable and suffers from droughts, floods, dust storms and earthquakes. Iran appears singular in that the more Anti-American the rulers, the more pro-American the people, although they would probably rally around the government should their nuclear sites be attacked. However, the regime is highly vulnerable to the cutting off of their supplies of gasoline, for which they have to import some 40%.

The regime is condemned for its economic mismanagement of both agriculture and industry, having diverted huge sums towards weaponry – so making it vulnerable to reduced food supplies, and perhaps revolution. A further weakness is that the country is obliged to import some 30% of its refined oil products. Iran employs around 30% in agriculture, compared to Turkey's 11.4% or Israel's 2.6%.

The previous table shows that of all the major players, Iran has the highest Drought Rating in the region of 555 but, as suggested earlier, the country has dammed water.

Like many countries in the Middle East, Iran has had a high birth rate with more than 25% under the age of 14 out of a population estimated at nearly 70 million in 2006. Apart from the energy business, many work in a bloated, inefficient state sector with the private activity being confined typically to small-scale farming, workshops, trade and services. Despite its $40 billion of foreign reserves, this has not been used to alleviate high unemployment, which has contributed to the president's poor showing in recent elections.

As we have seen, the probable drought in the area is liable to oblige Iran to seek moisture and food from perhaps the Tigris/Euphrates valley and Turkey. As a counter, a nuclear-armed Iran could threaten to strike Israel and hit the West economically through attempting to close the Hormuz waterway.

Apart from water shortages, Iran is highly vulnerable to a blockade on the exports of crude oil through an attack on Abadan and closing the Straits of Hormuz. There may also be internal dissent after radical Ayatollah Yazdi, the president's spiritual advisor, was deposed from the powerful Assembly of Experts. These Achilles Heels are perhaps reasons why President Bush has decided to increase the level of troops in Iraq in an attempt to isolate Iran's influence. However, it may take a conflict before Iran is obliged to acknowledge its weakness.

Syria

Syria has a history going back to the ancient civilisations associated with the great rivers Tigris and Euphrates. From the sixteenth century it, and the whole of Arabia including Egypt, was ruled by the Ottoman Empire from Istanbul. After the defeat of the Turks in the First World War, King Faisal of Mecca was given to believe that Syria would be ruled by one of his sons. However, at the Sykes-Picot Treaty of 1916 the area that is now Syria and Lebanon came under the control of France until independence in 1946.

It was in Damascus that the idea of the Arab Socialist Ba'ath Party was first formed. It espoused Arab nationalism, non-alignment and took inspiration from what was perceived as the positive values of Islam without too much notice being taken of its class divisions and lack of freedom. The Ba'ath Party was the inspiration behind Gamal Abdul Nasser's Egypt, Saddam Hussein's Iraq and Hafez al-Assad's Syria. All put great store on a powerful army largely equipped by Russia and manned by conscripts.

The first significant clash with Israel was during the Six-Day war in 1967, when the Jewish state captured the Golan Heights, a very significant feature that dominated much of north-east Israel, and the Yarmuk dam – a feeder river to the Jordan; unsurprisingly, Syria has made several attempts to redeem the Golan. Antipathy to Israel was the driving force that allied Syria to Iran after the 1979 revolution and the support of Hizbollah and Hammas with arms, training and funds. After the Lebanese civil war of 1976, Syria was very influential in the country until it was ejected in 2005.

The great Euphrates flows some 300 miles through Syria on its passage from Turkey to Iraq, and waters some 25% of what otherwise would be an arid and semi-desert country. Agriculture employs 30% of the work force on land irrigated by the Euphrates and from a narrow fertile coastal plain; even then, the country has difficulty in feeding the rapidly rising population with 37% being aged 14 years and younger. A further 25% of the GDP is made up by declining oil production whose value has been boosted by rising prices. Like other Ba'athist countries, Syria seems to believe that military spending takes precedence over the well-being of the people, including a proper understanding of the wise use of water. The Drought Rating is 420 – second to Egypt and probably also Iran.

There is little doubt that the mutual dislike of Israel and the drive to secure the Golan Heights would be enough to continue the alliance between Syria and a belligerent Iran, despite the former being Sunni and the latter Shi'a. This would be put to the test should Iran, supported by Syria and Al-qaeda, attempt to invade Iraq and Saudi Arabia to gain control of the Tigris, Euphrates and the major Gulf oil fields. At the same time, Syria might feel emboldened to try to re-take the Golan Heights from Israel in a co-ordinated effort with Hisbollah and Hammas. This would push the price of energy well above $180 a barrel of oil and serve the Jihadist cause of hurting the West economically.

Clearly, the main threat to Israel are the combined efforts of Syria, Hisbollah and Hammas under the potential nuclear umbrella of Iran. However, if water is the first objective then Mesopotamia and even Turkey could be the prime target. After all, an attempt to flatten Israel would only ensure a similar fate for Iran – a prospect even the Ayatollahs could hardly contemplate. Like Iran, Syria is vulnerable to any reduction in the Euphrates waters, as they were in 1991 when the eruption of Pinatubo reduced rainfall in the eastern Mediterranean. This caused Turkey to reduce the flow that nearly led to war – something that should be appreciated in Washington and Jerusalem.

The force ranged against Iran and Syria in the Middle East must be Israel itself and probably also Turkey.

Israel

Israel is a transplant of mainly European peoples who have regained much of their biblical lands but in the process have made mortal enemies in the Middle East. After the Diaspora in AD 80 there still remained pockets of Jews in Palestine and some formed themselves into Kibbutzim, co-operatives that held everything in common.

There had been many moves to create a state of Israel but the possibility became a reality when in 1917 the Balfour Declaration identified a home for the Jews in Palestine. After the Treaty of Lausanne in 1923 that divided up the Ottoman Empire, Britain held the region as a Mandate which allowed a considerable rise in the Jewish population – Jews fleeing persecution caused the numbers to rise from 84,000 in 1922, to 467,000 in 1940. At the same time much substandard land was tilled and the area under cultivation doubled. The rise in Jewry to nearly a third of the total population alarmed the Arabs who called for a general strike in 1937 and demanded independence; it was only put down by British troops and a rising force of 15,000 Zionists. In an attempt to restore order, the immigration quota was largely scaled back at a time when many Jews wanted to escape Hitler.

Following the United Nations declaration on the partition of Palestine, the Jewish state was formed in May 1948, triggering the first war against her neighbours; there were further conflicts in 1956, 1967, 1973 and 1982, of which 1967 was probably the most significant. In a six-day series of brilliant moves, Israel captured the Negev, the West Bank and the land around the Golan Heights; it set the basis for an agreement with Egypt and Jordan but still finds friction with the Palestinians, Syria and some sects in Lebanon.

There is a peace treaty with Jordan that regulates the use of the Jordan river, with both countries undertaking to protect the river and aquifers against pollution within their own jurisdiction. This has not prevented the 60 mile stretch of water from the Sea of Galilee to the Dead Sea from being heavily contaminated. **The amount of water available to each Palestinian is 320 cubic metres on average annually – a seventh of that consumed by the Israelis who use their water more efficiently**.

There is little doubt that Israel and Palestine are vulnerable to a reduction of water supplies caused by the ocean oscillations described earlier; these are now in a similar configuration to the drought in 1973 but with double the population.

Although Israel reported an annual deficiency of 500 million cubic metres of water, this could double by 2020 (Chapter 2 shows they are aware of the problem and are taking action).

This is the time to introduce the other likely ally, a country that has an abundance of water and could be powerfully involved in any potential surge of refugees from Central Asia (as suggested in Chapter 5).

Turkey

Until around 600 AD Anatolia, the land now occupied by Turkey, was under the control of the Byzantine Empire. From Constantinople, they ruled a considerable area from the Balkans then clockwise around the Mediterranean.

By the late seventh century the Byzantines were coming under pressure from the Muslim Arabs from the south,. At the same time the Empire was being infiltrated by Turkic peoples who hailed from east Central Asia, including Mongols, Manchurians and the Huns on their westward passage; present-day Turks still have many ethnic and linguistic links with Central Asian republics. The movements were consolidated by the Seljuk Turks based in Baghdad, most of whom became Muslims.

By the thirteenth and fourteenth centuries most of the Christian settlements in Anatolia had been overrun and even Constantinople was sometime under siege. This movement took form organised from the small province of Ottoman in north-west Anatolia under the dynamic leadership of Osman and his successors. The Ottomans crossed the Bosporus, moving north to the Balkans and south to Greece; they later consolidated their power in the rest of Anatolia after defeating Mongol forces. This movement is known as the Second Jihad and assumed the power of the Byzantine Empire after the capture of Constantinople in 1453. It was a remarkable achievement.

Eventually, the Ottoman Empire stretched from the gates of Vienna, through the Balkans and down through Mesopotamia, Arabia and Egypt. Their rule was relatively benign – providing the provinces paid their taxes. They were supported by a powerful army with elite corps of infantrymen, cavalry and later artillery. However, their power proved fallible when they were repelled by the Knights of Malta and defeated at the famous naval engagement of Lepanto in 1571. The Empire was starting to unravel.

The first to break away was Egypt, then Peloponnesia in the early nineteenth century, and the remainder of the Balkans in the decades that followed. In the First World War, the so-called 'Young Turks' led by Enver Pasha sided with Germany and, despite the Allied disaster at Gallipoli, they were gradually cleared out of Arabia, Palestine and Mesopotamia to near present-day borders.

It was a terrible defeat for a once-great nation but there arose one outstanding individual – Mustafa Kemal, the hero who won the Gallipoli campaign then later ejected the Greeks who tried to occupy Anatolia in 1922. This remarkable man orientated Turkey westwards. He changed the alphabet from Arabic to Roman, the school curriculum was based on that in France, he made the country secular and the law was taken away from the Sharia courts and Swiss laws substituted. For his achievements he was called Atatürk – father of the Turks. Although Turkey is now a multi-party state, the army still deems itself the keeper of the Atatürk heritage. It was responsible for taking power for a period in 1960 when politicians were in disarray.

Turkey is blessed with the most adequate rainfall in the Eastern Mediterranean and, through huge dams, controls the flow of the Tigris and Euphrates. Apart from forming anti-Soviet pacts in the 1960s, present-day Turkey has rejected pan-Islam and Arab nationalism and, like Iran, has been trying to regain its connections with the Turkic peoples of Central Asia.

Turkey has many links with Israel: both are westward-looking democracies with close military ties to the United States and both have formidable armed forces. Elsewhere, a gas pipeline has been constructed between Iran and Turkey and arrangements are in place to double mutual trade; with the rise in terrorism there is increasing common concern with Israel over the belligerency of Iran.

Turkey is, however, in a very strong position as it controls the two great rivers and has the lowest Drought Rating in the area. Like Israel it has concerns over Syria which complains over any restrictions in the flow of the Euphrates and supports the Kurds in their attempt to force a break-away state.

Iraq, formerly Mesopotamia

Iraq – the country between two great rivers and one of the great civilisations in the ancient world – is now at war with itself. Part of the Ottoman Empire until 1923 when, like Palestine, it was granted a British mandate until 1932, it then became independent under King Faisal. There were several assassination attempts on the Hashemite king until 1939 when the king died and the country was ruled by Rashid Ali, a pro-Nazi. Fearing a disruption of oil supplies, Britain re-occupied the country in 1941 until making it independent once again in 1947. Incited by Colonel Nasser of Egypt, the army staged a rebellion in 1958, the Faisal II was assassinated and the county was subsequently ruled by General Kassem, the first Ba'athist dictator.

Since then it has been ruled by despots, the only people seemingly able to control the Sunnis in the west, the Shi'as in the south and east and the Kurds in the north. At the time of writing it seems unlikely that the country will be able to remain an entity. But this is not for ethnic or religious reasons alone.

Iraq relies almost entirely for water from Turkey in the north and Turkey via Syria to the west. Although there have been complaints about controlling the flow through Syria, Turkey is making the situation less secure by building eight dams on the Tigris and thirteen on the Euphrates. Part of this is used for hydro-electric generation, but there are plans to divert water through tunnels to a two million hectare irrigation agricultural project in the south-east. Not only will Iraq and Syria receive less water but it will also likely have greater upstream contamination and less of the natural silt that has formerly stimulated farming. From this difficult scenario, the Middle East will have to contain another problem that will increasingly cause problems to most countries.

Unemployment

Water is not the only problem facing Middle Eastern governments: the International Labour Organization, based in Geneva, reports that **unemployment in the Middle East North African group (MENA) is the highest in the world at 13.2% – even greater than sub-Saharan Africa**. MENA has the lowest women's employment at in the world 23.5% and the secretary-general of the Arab League estimates the total number of unemployed is 22 million, of whom 60% are youths. These aimless people must be a potential cause for revolutions to governments in the region and, if radicalised, a grave danger to the West.

Seven scenarios for the region

From the above, one can now identify at least seven scenarios as to how the problems and conflicts in the area might be resolved:

Scenario one: peace through exchanging know-how for water and employment

All the countries considered earlier, except Iran, and many others are members of the Arab League formed in 1945 to co-ordinate economic, health and social affairs and communications. From its base in Cairo it is an influential body. As water and unemployment affect all the participants, perhaps this is the body to initiate a programme with Israel, so in exchange for peace their young people could learn the skills in hydrology that could radically increase the ability of the Arab countries to increase their prosperity.

Scenario two: the Bush strategy in Iraq may succeed

It is a truism that when all the supposed experts agree on an outcome the basis for success possibly lies elsewhere. There is evidence that the Coalition forces are succeeding in isolating the dissidents – one that succeeded in the Malayan Emergency of the 1950s. Under the command of General Sir Gerald Templer, the allied forces progressively isolated trouble spots and converted these into conflict-free areas. This starved the communists of their support and supplies.

Just recently the oil city of Mosul has started to become secure after the leading trouble-maker and his supporters were removed and the local militia helped to restore primary services. No one claims that Mosul will be untroubled in the future but the American commander General Petraeus is gradually weaning away the local headmen from supporting violence and isolating Iranian and Syrian influence.

Scenario three: an Israeli/US air attack on the Iranian nuclear facilities

This has been a distinct possibility ever since Iran dismissed the UN nuclear inspectors. However, with the deployment of Tor-M1 SAMs, an attack other than by stealth aircraft and deep penetration bombs is unlikely to succeed. Israel is technically capable of carrying out such a mission, but the result is only likely to delay, not abort, the programme – because of the close association of Iran with North Korea. (It should be noted that the nuclear programme has been recently downgraded in importance by US Intelligence.)

In reply Iran could attempt to block the Strait of Hormuz with mines, Silkworm sea-skimming missiles and possibly kamikaze-type attacks on shipping with fast motor boats. This would effectively raise the price of oil but could be counter-productive should allied sea and air forces reply by blocking Iran's imports and exports, attacking the Abadan oil refinery and knocking-out military installations.

Scenario four: a combined attack by Syria, Hamas and Hisbollah with Iran on Israel

This could be a possibility that might have some chance of success without exposing Iran to a nuclear bombardment. Initially the two terrorist groups could attack, supported by firing the short-range Ograb rockets. Next, Iran could stretch defence forces further by discharging Shahab 4 missiles with conventional warheads. Finally, Syria could attack the Golan Heights. Although Israel has already taken counter-measures against these forms of attack, a settlement should be possible along the lines suggested in Scenario One.

Scenario five: an attempt to harm the West economically by trying to block the Strait of Hormuz with harassing attacks

It is reported that Al-Qaeda, and presumably Iran, have been studying how a small nation like Vietnam could defeat a large and powerful country. Selective attacks on allied vessels might force the oil price well above $180 a barrel – a level that would start damaging Western economies. This could force a response similar to Scenario Two, but if the Iranians were selective in their targets it could be difficult to argue for a full-scale response.

Scenario six: to avoid internal riots Iran might attempt to secure the Kuwait oil fields

Thus giving them additional revenue and enough water through desalination plants. As suggested earlier, potential drought and the threat to petroleum supplies is Iran's prime Achilles Heel. They could use their water more intelligently and have enough oil to run desalination plants cheaply, but this would leave them even more vulnerable to attack should they show aggression.

Scenario seven: the drought becomes so severe that Iran, with the help of the Shi'a Iraqis, tries to occupy Mesopotamia and threatens Turkey with a nuclear attack should they restrict the river flows

This would be a totally contrarian view of Iran's predicament. While everybody thinks Israel will be the target, the real aim may actually be for Iran to occupy Iraq and possibly even Turkey.

This would certainly demand a US response and possibly also a resolution of the Palestinian/Iraqi question through an alliance of the major Sunni countries. Any advance by Iran into Iraq would seriously concern Saudi Arabia, Kuwait, Egypt, Jordan and possibly even the Palestinians. The Sunni states might find it attractive to create a non-Ba'ath federation with the backing of the US as a shield against Iran. As part of the settlement Saudi Arabia might fund the partition of Iraq, find a homeland for displaced Palestinians and settle the Kurdish KKK question. As suggested earlier, the deal could also include the supply of Israeli technology and Turkish water.

This last scenario could achieve a number of objectives:

1. Iran would have her water and establish some sort of union with the Iraqi Shi'as; after a while the latter might not appreciate the stifling and inefficient embrace of the Sharia Law and could lead to the removal of the clerical regime.

2. The Arab Sunni states would achieve some sort of stability and security after absorbing some Palestinians. Probably the country having the greatest disquiet would be Saudi Arabia surrounded on two sides by Shi'as but the Sunni Treaty could reduce their concerns.

3. Turkey holds the key to Syria being obliged to drop the Ba'ath regime in return for a guaranteed flow of the Euphrates. She might also be prepared to acknowledge an independent Kurdestan as part of the settlement.

4. Israel would have to trade her agricultural expertise as part of the settlement and would be the sole nuclear power supporting the Sunni states against any Shi'a aggression. As suggested, her greatest contribution would be to help the Arab people to vastly improve their economies.

5. The United States and her coalition partners could justify their invasion of Iraq as the key to the settlement and defence of the West's oil supplies.

References

- *A Peace to End All Peace*, by David Fromkin (Phoenix Books, 2000)

- *Browning Newsletter*, Fraser Publishing Co, PO Box 404, Burlington Vermont 05402

- *Countdown to Crisis*, by Kenneth R. Timmerman (Three Rivers Press, 2006)

- *Decline and Fall of the Ottoman Empire, The* by Alan Palmer (John Murray, 1992)

- *Encyclopedia Britannica*

- *Future Storm*, by William Houston and Robin Griffiths (Harriman House, 2006)

- *Iran Under the Ayatollahs*, by Dilip Hiro (Routledge & Kegan Paul, 1985)

- *Looming Crisis of Water in the Middle East, The*, by Dr Nimrod Raphael (MEMRI, 2003)

- *Turkey: A Short History*, by Roderic H. Davidson (Eothaen Press, 1988)

- *Turkish Foreign Policy*, by Clement H. Doss (Eothaen Press, 1992)

- www.StrategicReview.com October 12th 2006

- *Unemployment in the Middle East – Causes and consequences*, by Dr Nimrod Raphael (MEMRI, 2006)

- *Water: The International Crisis*, by Robin Clarke (Earthscan, 2003)

- www.halkinservices.co.uk Weekly Letter, October 12th 2006

- *When the Rivers Run Dry*, by Fred Pearce (Beacon Press, 2006)

- *The World Factbook*

7

Potential for Conflicts over Water in the East

Summary

Of the many factors determining instability in the East, water is likely to become dominant. The previous chapter considered conflicts over shared river basins in the Middle East; this chapter will identify how growing climatic problems in Pakistan, China and North Korea, all nuclear-armed countries, could engulf them in conflicts and mass migrations.

Those most at risk from China are Burma and Vietnam, from Pakistan is the East Punjab and from North Korea its southern neighbour. Any attempt by China to control Burma could bring conflict with India. New alliances will be formed to include the English-speaking peoples, India and Japan. The scenarios at the chapter end show how these patterns could evolve

Introduction

While the developed world seemed to be focusing entirely on a climate driven by man-made gasses, Chapter One explained how the great oceans are continuing to oscillate between being unusually warm or cool as they have for millions of years; at the same time the tropics are expanding to cause drought in sensitive areas. Now the Atlantic will be particularly warm until the 2020s and at the same time the Pacific is becoming unusually cool. This implies that **if there is to be a conflict over water it will occur within the next ten or so years.**

A cooler Pacific forces the rain belts further south to make Northern China, Korea and Central Asia unusually dry with extremes of hot and cold; major volcanic eruptions could only make conditions worse. Most of these countries have poor water management demanding a very high proportion of their population engaged on the land; the one exception is South Korea that has efficiencies approaching the West.

Unfortunately all these countries have experienced a huge rise in their population over the previously benign climatic period. This increases the risk of civil unrest or revolution should water shortages and the high price of commodities force a much lower standard of living – even starvation. The famine of 1958-61 in China, made much worse by Mao's policy of exporting food, forced 38 million into starvation. With these oscillations prevailing for up to two decades, there could be serious consequences internally and for armed conflict abroad over water.

Drought Rating

To assess those countries likely to be most affected, the following table sets out a series of factors that could guide us to the water deficit nations and those likely to be targets for aggression should there be failures in water supply.

The aim is to establish a nation Drought Rating based on the population of eight countries. This is then modified depending upon the efficiency of agriculture and liability for drought.

- First there is a calculation of the numbers of people per square kilometre of arable land, which provides a basic assessment of the agricultural support available should they have to feed themselves.

- The next factor is the efficiency of agricultural water use based on the population employed in farming, divided into percentage bands.

- The third is the probability of water shortage based on the oscillations. The final Drought Rating provides a relative assessment of each country to these shortages.

Country	Land K.sq.Km	Arable %	Population Million	Pop/sq Km	Efficiency Basis A	Drought Basis B	**Drought Rating**
Burma	657	14.9	47.3	483	3	0.66	1886
China	9326	14.8	1.31bn	942	3	1	2827
India	2973	48.8	1.1bn	758	3	1	2275
Indonesia	1826	11	235	1169	3	0.66	2315
N.Korea	120.4	22.4	23.1	858	3	1.3	3346
S Korea	98.1	16.6	48.8	2993	1/3	1.3	1297
Pakistan	779	24.4	165	873	3	1.3	3403
Vietnam	325	20.1	84.4	1292	3	0.66	2559

Basis A: efficiency rating – percentage of population in agriculture

Between 2-5% – Million population/sq km divided by   8

Between 5-15% – Million population/sq km divided by   3

Between 15-30% – Million population/sq km divided by   1

Above 30% – Million population/sq km multiply by   3

Basis B: for drought rating – see Chapter 1

Drought very likely – multiplier for million population/sq km   1.33

Drought likely – multiplier for million population/sq km   1

Drought unlikely – multiplier for million population/sq km   0.66

Material taken from CIA Factbook/geos

We can now divide the major countries in Asia between:

- Those with a high vulnerability to drought: *China, North Korea and Pakistan.*

- Those that might be attractive, not only as a source of water but also to provide access to strategic materials or to new oceans: *Burma, Kashmir, South Korea and Vietnam.*

First, an assessment of the primary deficiency countries.

Water deficient countries

China

China, together with Egypt, Mesopotamia and along the Indus, is one of the great cradles of civilisation. For centuries China has been blessed by the flow of two great rivers: the Yangtze and the Hwang Ho or Yellow River. The former takes its source from deep in the eastern Himalayas, the latter in the mountains bordering the Gobi Desert. From these two rivers human settlements stretch back to 7000 BC where over time they grew millet and rice, fashioned copper tools and practised medicine.

Over the course of history China has been controlled centrally by reigning dynasties which have dominated the country for well over 2000 years. The Emperors have been either home-grown or from northern invaders, which make the communists the first Chinese rulers for around 500 years. Sometimes these monarchs have divided the country north and south, as in the time of Ghengis Khan and his grandson Kubla Khan.

Quite early on, emperors ruled through a civil service where a competitive entrance was held based on Confucian teaching, a custom that ensured only the elite managed the country. This has now changed so that the bureaucracy is largely in the hands of the army or Party, where there is ample opportunity for corruption; it also suffers the fatal flaw that, in the absence of a free media, no official can report bad news if they want to keep their job. The borders of China have varied over the centuries depending upon the mood of the emperor. Those now in power look back in time before the 1840s when the country controlled much of Central Asia, Burma, Tibet, Laos, Cambodia and Vietnam. Since then the borders have been contained similarly to the present-day except for Tibet.

In the twentieth century the rule changed with the Revolution of Sun Yat-sen in October 1910 (the tenth of the tenth of the tenth). This deposed the Manchu monarchy and a republic was declared, which in due course was managed by the Kuomintang Party. Despite commanding large armies, they were ineffective in stopping the brutal invasion by Japan in the 1930s, and the country was occupied until 1945. There followed a civil war in which the Communists, led by Mao Tse-Tung and supported by the Kremlin, gained military domination until declaring the new state in October 1949.

Mao's drive to become a world power seemingly at the expense of 90 million of his own people – 38 million alone by starvation – puts him in the forefront of human monsters, even by the standards of some brutal emperors. His rule was total and he apparently took pleasure is ridding himself of anyone that had caused him the least disagreement or slight. Mao died in 1976 to be succeeded by Deng Xiaoping who, either by accident or design, gradually allowed the bar to private enterprise to unwind and welcomed the infusion of foreign capital. By the twenty-first century, China was attracting foreign manufacturing firms to a low-cost and seemingly reliable environment; there was also the lure of a potential market of over a billion people with rising affluence.

China's growth at around 10% a year, 2% more than its nearest rivals India and Singapore, has dazzled the world. However, there are a number of problems that could affect its future, including the increasing desertification described in Chapter 1.

First the banks: formed primarily to finance state-owned industries, these have an increasing number of bad debts and at the same time have excessive cash from dollars converted into yuan from exporting firms. This has allowed excess credit to finance speculation in housing and other excesses. Any reversals could prove fatal to further growth.

Next, although central direction could be effective for a while to launch and manage large infrastructure road, rail and air projects, there is no feed-back through an independent media or any form of democracy if things go wrong. This means that the only way people are able to protest against gross wastage, or the state riding roughshod over individuals, will be through unrest and riots.

In 2002, 100,000 factory hands rioted and in 2004 another 100,000 protested violently that land had been confiscated without compensation to build a hydro-electric plant. Another example, **should the Yellow River be increasingly unable to support a huge proportion of the population, the unrest could become revolutionary**.

The source of the Hwang (or Yellow River) is a series of natural reservoirs, of which Lakes Gyaning and Ngoring are the largest. It flows eastwards, north through Inner Mongolia then south through Shanxi Province before reaching the northern plains where it flow north-east to the Bohai Sea.

It is called the Yellow River because it carries a vast tonnage of loess that, like the Nile, has fertilised the lower plains for centuries. However, sources are running dry through the advance of the Gobi Desert and a reduction in rainfall – most likely due to the Pacific Oscillation described earlier. The Chinese authorities must perceive dust storms as a major potential threat to the Beijing Olympics.

This is serious because **China has some of the lowest per-capita water supplies in the world** and suffers from uneven distribution. Northern China is home to 43% of the population but has only 14% of the water. This means that some half a billion people depend upon the main wheat growing area in the world, but that water is running out.

Wheat output increased from 90 million tons in 1950, to 292 million tons in 1998 – the equivalent to the entire output of Canada. Since 2000, Diagram 8 shows how the wheat stocks have declined by two thirds since 2000, through a combination of increasing desertification, reduction of cropland and capricious or polluted water supplies. This is starting to generate huge deficits that, as Chapter 3 argued, there will be few countries able to make up the difference.

Diagram 8. Carry-over stocks of Wheat 1960-2006

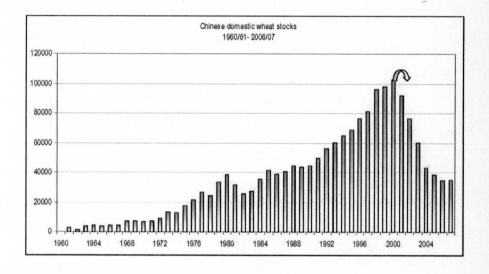

Source: Diapason

The population along the Yellow River has tripled since the 1950s to service the rapid industrialisation under Mao, so the river has become progressively polluted. Water abstraction is so great that in some years a bare trickle reaches the sea by the new city of Zhengzhou. Because of this, water is being pumped from aquifers that are only partly replenished every year. Now boreholes have to be sunk more deeply – some to half a mile around Beijing. **The capital is also threatened by deserts that have combined and are now encroaching to within 150 miles**.

Lower down the Yellow River, the once fertile plain is in danger of becoming a dust bowl with the problem of toxic dust storms covering huge areas – at times reaching

North America. The authorities are concerned about the occasional flooding that would be a disaster for the millions of people who live close to the river, prompting extensive work on levees that rise well above the land. One is reminded how the Aral Sea became a toxic wasteland after the Soviets diverted the great rivers of Syr Darya and Amu Darya in order to grow cotton.

Unfortunately the Yellow River is not alone. China is suffering what is known as the Japan Syndrome. Like Japan, South Korea and Taiwan, **China is losing arable land (18% in five years) through conversion into towns, industrial areas, roads and car parks**. It is also losing pasture through over-grazing that has accelerated desertification to the tune of 1,400 sq miles/year.

Now **400 of China's 600 cities are suffering from water shortages**; they are making up the difference by pumping from aquifers that themselves are becoming much dryer with only one third being replenished in a year. One such is the drought reported in the south-western region of Chongqing, where in late summer 2006 there had been no rain for more than 70 days and two-thirds of the rivers had dried up rendering crop failures from valuable farmland and the death of cattle. In some areas residents of some towns were obliged to walk over a mile to draw water.

In southern China the Yangtze, the third longest river in the world, is polluted with industrial and agricultural waste and there are fears that by 2011 it will be unable to sustain marine, much less human life; reports show that around 400 million people have no access to unpolluted water – the toxicity has spread. *The Economist* reports that Taihu, the third largest lake in the country, is now totally polluted with a deadly algae that is taking a terrible toll on the surrounding area. Upstream, the Three Gorges Dam, the world's largest and designed to open up the interior to shipping, is in trouble from upstream silting and pollution. In addition there are doubts about its security for there are increasing concerns about erosion of the hillsides and there are contingency plans to relocate four million people. China aims to transfer water from the great rivers of the south to the north at very considerable expense, but this could only add to the woes of the south.

The great leaps forward initiated first by Mao then more constructively by Deng have created a growth at any cost that could probably not have been possible in a democracy but, like Hitler's Germany in the early 1930s, have created immediate results. Unfortunately for China her fortunes do not depend upon herself but to a large extent the US. **Should America suffer a downturn, all the problems of centralisation, pollution, water shortages, the loss of agricultural land, the poor female/male ratio and bad debts in the banking system could surface.**

The Drought Rating table shows an estimate of China's vulnerability compared to other countries. With a Drought Rating of 2827 it ranks third with North Korea and Pakistan as the country most at risk of dangers of revolution and from the anticipated drought and increased deaths from waterborne diseases. Cancer experts estimate that 70% of the two million deaths from this disease were pollution related. All these factors places at risk surplus counties, such as Vietnam and Burma, from forced appropriation.

North Korea

North Korea has rightly been much in the news for its detonation of a nuclear device but, one suspects, this is possibly to divert attention from its real vulnerability: its inefficient agriculture. Unfortunately this water is largely wasted and any serious shortages could provide at least one reason for another invasion of the south.

The Korean Peninsula was an independent kingdom for much of its history until it was invaded and occupied by Japan at the end of the Russo-Japanese War in the early years of the twentieth century. After Japan's defeat in 1945, the Peninsula was split, the north coming under the communist control of Kim Il Sung and the US-backed republic in the south with the division along the 38th Parallel. The north under Kim, and then his son, remain a communist state despite others such as Yugoslavia, China and then Russia, and even Albania, attempting to introduce forms of democracy and capitalism.

This doctrine has concentrated its economy on heavy industry and armaments, while leaving it vulnerable to drought and its inefficient farming; 34% of its working population are working on the land, which helps to give it the worst Drought Rating of any of the countries analysed. Its inability to use water efficiently probably contributed to its decision to invade the south in 1950.

Pakistan

Pakistan may, at first sight, seem an odd bedfellow with China and North Korea but, like the others, it is extremely vulnerable to drought – particularly to the ocean oscillations described earlier. Although the source of the mighty Indus rises north in the country, the rivers Ravi, Beas, Sutlej, Jhelum and Chenoa all pass through India and there are running disputes over how much abstraction can be taken upstream.

The Partition of India demanded by Jinnah in 1947 was supposed to have included the Muslim-dominant state of Kashmir but it remained part of India, despite being the cause of wars in 1947, 1965 and 1971 (the latter conflict gave independence to Bangladesh, previously East Pakistan). More recently it is believed that China gave Pakistan help with its nuclear weapons and has supplied frigates to equal the numbers commissioned by India.

With a Drought Rating of 3403, Pakistan has the additional problem of saline contamination of the soil that reduces the available arable land much further. Like other major countries in Asia it has much to fear from drought and, with only 20% of the population having access to clean water, conflicts with India seem bound to increase. Now, armed with nuclear weapons and becoming increasingly unstable politically, it could be tempted to regain what many believed it lost in Partition while India's attention is directed elsewhere.

Now to turn to the primary water surplus countries.

Water surplus countries

Burma (Myanmar)

Burma (or Myanmar) was, for several centuries, part of the Chinese empire that, before the Opium Wars of the 1840s, stretched nearly as far west as the Caspian Sea. After that it became a British Protectorate governed mostly from India, until it gained independence after the Second World War, largely through the leadership of Aung San. Following his assassination in 1947, the country has been ruled by a military junta that has refused any form of democracy and has repressed any efforts of the movement that won overwhelming support in an election. Not unlike North Korea, Burma has remained a distant and remote country regarded by many in the West as a pariah. Close neighbours India and China have become increasingly concerned about its stability – the democracy leader Aung San Suu Kyi was educated in India before going to Oxford and her movement is supported by India.

However, **the attraction of Burma for a potential predator is the abundance of water from the great Irrawaddy**, which has two sources that are primarily within Burma and therefore cannot be disrupted by China. There is another river, the Salween, that rises in the Chinese province of Xinjiang, and enters Burma at the eastern half of the country before discharging into the sea to the east of Rangoon.

What makes Burma doubly attractive for an occupier is that it is resource-rich, having oil and minerals that are being under-utilised through socialism, incompetence and corruption. This forces 70% of its people to work on the land in the very extensive paddy fields that cover the delta. The Chinese have built a four-lane road to Burma and would find Rangoon an attractive port on the Andaman Sea. Any incursion by China is most likely to be resisted by India.

India

India as a subcontinent has been, like China, one of the great centres of civilisation in the Indus valley through which invaders, such as Alexander and subsequently the

Mughals, have passed. The British first foothold was in Bengal but they effectively gained control from the French in the latter part of the eighteenth century and became the ruling power until independence and partition in 1947.

The Drought Rating table shows that of all the eastern countries, India has nearly half its land available for agriculture which means, providing the summer monsoon does not fail, the country should have a great capacity for feeding itself, helped by water delivered from major damming of the great rivers. However, this means a considerable amount is lost through evaporation, conduits lose even more, so that some ninety percent of fresh water goes to wasteful methods of irrigation (70% is the usual ratio). This leaves much less for domestic consumption which, if people are wise, they boil before drinking. Even these measures do not provide portions of a burgeoning population with food and fresh water.

In many dry areas, such as Gujarat and Rajasthan, on the West coast farmers have sunk bore holes hundreds of feet down to access non-replaceable water in aquifers; even if water is adequate much of it is lost thought wasteful farming methods. It is hoped the damming of the Narmada River will give some respite from the drought, but it will be fed from open canals that will cause extensive evaporation. Further north, **although the Ganges rises in Nepal, and part of the Brahmaputra in China, India does control much of its own water**. Armed with atomic weapons, and with its huge population, India is an unlikely target for a predator, unless the potential foes are acting in concert.

For example, the leaders of China could become so frightened by the possibility of revolution that they invade Burma to relieve the food shortages. India has already had disputes with China over a large part of Arunachal Pradesh in the north-east and control over the source of the Brahmaputra, so that any invasion of Burma is likely to be strenuously resisted given the potential advantages to the occupier. Given the closeness of China to Pakistan, the two countries could serve their own ends by joint action.

Vietnam

Vietnam, like Burma, was once part of China until the 1840s when it came under French control and remained so until after the Second World War when it proclaimed independence; this was resisted by the French until 1954, when it was formally divided between north and south. The country was finally united in 1973 under the communist north that inhibited development, but latterly the authorities have encouraged export-driven industries.

In the beneficial oscillations of the La Nina, **Vietnam is well supplied with moisture for agriculture, which employs 57% of its population**. It is watered by the Mekong River that rises in China and forms the border with Thailand for much of its passage, although there have been disputes over the level of abstraction. On the Drought Rating, Vietnam fares just worse than Pakistan and ranks below Burma as a target for invasion. Despite this being once part of China, its military past would make it a much tougher nut for China to target.

Indonesia

Indonesia is huge country sprawling from Sumatra in the west to Irian Jaya (New Guinea) in the east; with 17,508 islands of which 6,000 are inhabited. It is home to some quarter of all Muslims. It was originally colonised by the Dutch early in the seventeenth century, was occupied by Japan during the Second World War, and achieved independence in 1949. Since then the country tried to occupy Brunei, and there is an ongoing disagreement over East Timor – this was formerly occupied by Portugal and now has independence supervised by Australia.

The Dutch were first attracted to the area by its richness in oil, energy, mining, coal, timber and precious metal resources. They also had to deal with the most seismically active area in the world, where two of the largest volcanoes erupted in modern times: Tambora in 1815 and Krakatoa in 1883. The western island Sumatra was also badly devastated by the tsunami of 2004, along with many countries in the Indian Ocean. Indonesia is benefiting from the present Pacific Oscillations with adequate rainfall that would make it an obvious target for refugees.

South Korea

South Korea has a similar history to the North until its partition in 1948 and its invasion in 1950. Since the 38th parallel was re-established in 1953, the growth of the country has been remarkable, completely outperforming the North. Even in agriculture, and with seemingly a similar hydraulic profile, their efficiency is such that only 6.4% are employed in agriculture. This gives it the lowest Drought Rating of any of the countries analysed, despite the propensity for drought conditions it shares with neighbouring countries. Its prosperity also makes it an attractive target for the North should they believe that American power would be dispersed elsewhere.

Alternative scenarios

Taking into account the hydrological strengths and weaknesses of the countries analysed, there is a rising probability of conflicts over water that could be co-ordinated in order to catch the water surplus countries at their weakest. These are set out under three levels of drought severity.

Level One

At Level One: for at least 40 years, Asia has suffered a net deficit in food production ameliorated by supplies primarily from the United States. **Despite the Green Revolution that improved crops, irrigation and farming methods, the agricultural output has not kept up with the growth of population**. Up to early in the twenty-first century the US could support these countries but, as earlier chapters have suggested, the Oscillations and increasing tropics have turned against North America and there may be little surplus.

At this level the drought caused by the La Nina is relatively mild, so that although the Yellow River remains a problem, China could still possibly feed herself by additional rewards to farmers. This problem must be of grave concern to the communist rulers who must also be aware of the potential for revolution. One could expect China to make contingencies for diverting the attention of the US while plans are being made to occupy possibly Burma in conjunction with action from Pakistan and North Korea. Unfortunately there will be little time to introduce Israeli-type agricultural reforms to deter conflict.

Level Two

At Level Two, it will be evident to the outside world that China, North Korea and Pakistan are suffering distress from water and food shortages. There is little doubt this will be alerting India and her allies to increase military preparedness and to re-arm. This will not just concern India but also Japan, the US and her allies. This could become more evident after the 2008 Olympic Games in 2008.

Level Three

At Level Three, there is a co-ordinated invasion of Burma, East Punjab and South Korea that may include action by Iran to divert US ground forces. Iran will initially be the greatest concern to the US over oil supplies, but very soon the East will become the dominant theatre.

The situation could encourage Japan to arm herself with nuclear weapons from their abundant store of plutonium; it might also become the lead nation to defy the North Koreans. A new coalition will be set up by the allies to support India with sea and air forces. With many of the contestants armed with nuclear weapons, the outcome could become extremely serious. One option would be for China to retaliate on the West by detonating a nuclear weapon in the stratosphere to disrupt the West's superiority in communications and satellite-led weapons.

How would Russia respond? It is bordered by China to the east and the conflicts to the south and may suffer from an influx of refugees. It is difficult to see it becoming part of the Axis and threatening the Atlantic as in the Cold War. It could even take the opportunity to industrialise with the help of France and Germany – both states receiving cheap energy in return.

References

- CIA factsheet/geos

- *Climate and Food Security*, by the American Foundation (International Rice Institute, 1989)

- *Encyclopedia Britannica*

- *Future Storm*, by William Houston and Robin Griffiths (Harriman House, 2006)

- *Mao*, by Jung Chang and Jon Halliday (Vintage Books, 2005)

- *Newsweek*, June 4th 2007

- *New York Times*

- *Outgrowing the Earth*, by Lester Brown (Earthscan, 2005)

8

Water and Technology

Summary

It is often argued that it requires a crisis to bring about change, and surely the prospect that millions of people might be without food and water in the next few years is such a moment. The same is true of innovation and in Chapters 2 and 3 we suggested measures that must be taken now to save even some of the arable land from being wasted.

Much of the work to revive overstretched soil has to be manual, but technology can also help. In this chapter we sketch out innovations that could relieve at least some of the water shortages and suggest how a fuel such as hydrogen may find a place from the tyranny of oil price rises. We can also observe that ground-breaking technologies, such as nanotechnology, tend to be advanced in times of crisis – to find commercial applications later.

Introduction

Chapter 2 showed how the Israelis are mastering the limitations of water supply, but even they have not overcome the technique of creating fresh water cheaply. In the meantime we have to learn about the technology of desalinisation and the associated sources of power.

Desalinisation

Desalinisation is a technology that is at the heart of water procurement – the basic techniques of evaporation and reverse osmosis were touched on in Chapter 2.

Although the processes remain the same, the technology is advancing.

The conventional evaporating technique seeks to use either electric power or fossil fuel to evaporate salt water under a partial vacuum at a cost reckoned to be ten times that of fresh water piped from a dam. The technique uses a series of evaporations depending upon the required quality of the output.

Passarell Process

One development is the Passarell Process that is starting to be used in California at a cost, it is claimed, of $800/acre foot of distilled water (1 acre/ft is equivalent to 326,000 gallons). This is claimed to be two to four times as economical to run as competitive units.

Diagram 10. Passarell Desalinisation Process

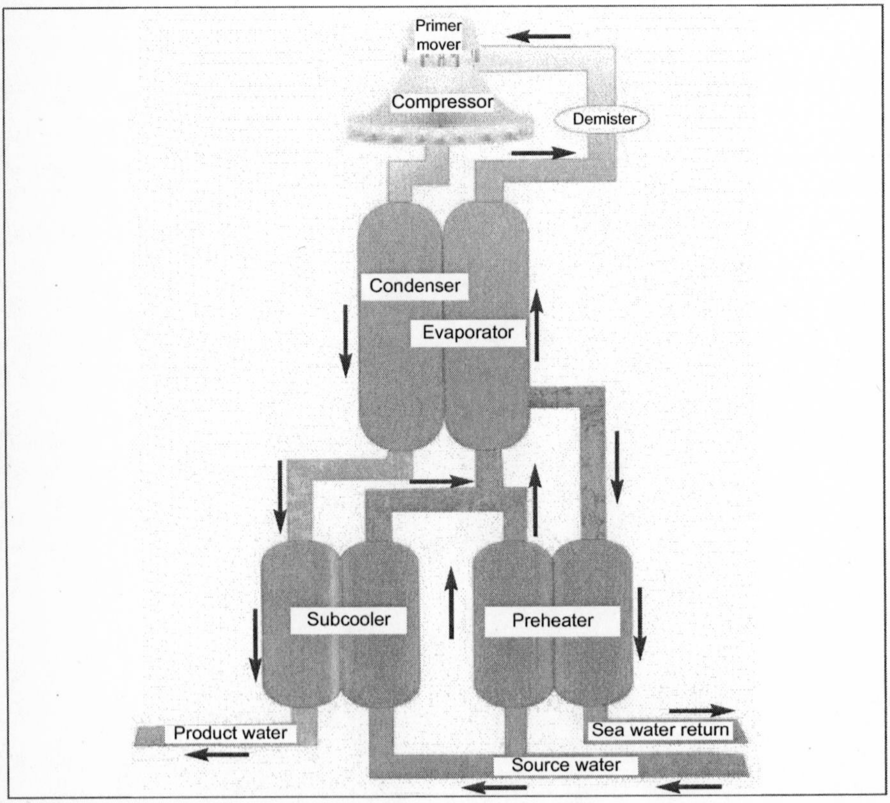

Source: Water Desalination International

The diagram shows the layout of the evaporator column of 33 feet – the length of a column of water to support the equivalent column of air at sea level – which has a vacuum at the top. This is the condition for water to evaporate, the vapour passes through a demister to remove residual solids before entering a compressor that, downstream, accentuates the vacuum and accelerates evaporation. The heated vapour is passed to the condenser and subsequently the sub-cooler, where heat is transferred to the incoming brine; this is then passed to the evaporator to accelerate the process. The lower than usual salt content of the returning brine is designed to get around some of the disadvantages of other desalinisation plants, where the high concentration of brine returned to the sea damages the ecology.

Reverse osmosis

The reverse osmosis process (touched on in Chapter 2) forces salt water through several membranes in series to achieve the required level of potability. Livermore National Laboratories now claim they have derived a more efficient system using nanotechnology.

This is a branch of a number of different technologies dealing with a nanometre (a billionth part of a metre – or the width of around six hydrogen atoms). The process assembles individual molecules in accordance with a pre-programmed series to fabricate the desired article. The process is currently used for such things as surface coatings or skin creams, but now it is being applied to desalination.

By rolling sheets of carbon atoms very tightly, scientists have produced apertures seven water atoms apart that, contrary to theory, accelerate the flow through electrostatically charged sheets. These retain the salt atoms and the fresh water passes through the diaphragm at a cost, it is claimed, of a 75% reduction of power compared to a standard reverse osmosis plant.

All desalination needs energy that, in the absence of cheap fossil fuel, may come from power sources at present under development. The most important of these are cold fusion, fuel cells, and solar power.

Cold fusion

Like the Philosopher's Stone of old that attempted to convert base metals into gold, the nuclear age hopes to generate power from fusing the atoms of deuterium (heavy water). Employing the process that drives the sun, heat is released when the deuterium is subjected to very high temperatures and pressure, with the reaction producing tritium, helium and radiation. A similar reaction is carried out in a fusion bomb, but the trigger is a fission device – something hardly desirable for peaceful use. There are two approaches. One is a very long-term project aiming to reproduce the high temperatures in a torus, an ultra high-speed particle generator, currently being built in France. The other aims to produce the conditions in a laboratory.

The first attempt was made by two researchers, Fleischmann and Pons, in March 1989, using a palladium electrode immersed in deuterium to produce above average heat, but none of the other expected side effects appeared to be present. The experiment could not be replicated by other scientists so it was deemed a programme unworthy for US federal funding.

Further experiments placed palladium electrodes only nanometres apart in deuterium solution. The intention was that enough colliding heavy water atoms would produce heat accompanied by either a tritium (triple hydrogen) or helium atom and, in some reactions, gamma rays. However, the palladium cathode was subject to cracking and melting, and there is presently no known way of generating heat from gamma rays.

It is hoped that the 'hot spots' generated by the deuterium and palladium can be replicated and controlled. If at the same time, the cathode deterioration can be overcome, there is a real opportunity to produce electricity initially up to a megawatt of power. There is also the possibility of scaling down these devices into really quite small packages.

Hydrogen and the fuel cell

The possibility of using hydrogen, the lightest of all elements as a fuel, only became a reality with the space programme. When burnt with oxygen, hydrogen provides the most powerful rocket impulse – far outweighing other propellants. Although widely used industrially, only more recently has its input for a fuel cell become a real possibility.

As we have seen, an isotope of this remarkable element is not only the basis for cold fusion, it is being actively developed as a commercial fuel with an energy content of 52,000 btus/lb – far in excess of its fossil competitors. In this environmentally conscious age, it burns cleanly with oxygen in the production of water; when burnt with air, there are some associated nitrogen compounds that can cause explosions unless the ratios are very carefully controlled.

Although hydrogen can be produced from water, biomass and coal, over 95% of all the hydrogen is made by steam reforming as natural gas – a chemical process whereby one molecule is changed into another having different properties. However, if hydrogen is to extend its industrial role it could be formed by electrolysing water; when a current is passed through an electrolyte, hydrogen is attracted to the cathode and oxygen to the anode. Usually this is powered either by nuclear fuel, hydro-electricity or, as we shall see later, solar power.

A research team at Perdue University, Indiana, USA has discovered another method that could revolutionise the conveyance and use of hydrogen. This employs a reaction of water with an aluminium alloy, which is the equivalent of electrolysing water described earlier. Currently, around 42 million tons of hydrogen are produced every year – most of it being converted to produce ammonia for fertilisers. As a gas it needs to be transported at high pressure to compact this exceptionally versatile element.

Unless it is formed as part of a continuous process, hydrogen is transported in cylinder stacks at pressures of 3381 pounds/square inch (around 230 atmospheres); it is estimated that a trailer could deliver the gasoline equivalent at a cost upwards or $1.20 a gallon depending upon upstream items such as generated electricity, demineralising and so on. It then has to be conveyed to a vehicle's high pressure cylinder through a suitable hose. Once onboard it can be used in a modified internal combustion engine or in a fuel cell (to be considered later).

The National Hydrogen Association naturally boosts the advantages of their gas by suggesting that the production process uses only a third of the amount of water to electrolyse the equivalent volume of fossil fuels. If the costs of hydrogen delivery are as set out earlier, the Association reports that the cost of a hybrid-driven gasoline vehicle would be the same as one driven by a fuel cell, although the capital cost would be higher. The question of safety and security of supply then arises.

The cost of transport, its high pressure storage and its natural flammability could dissuade drivers from switching to hydrogen, providing oil is around $80 per barrel; this could change should the gas be generated from water and the aluminium alloy described earlier. However, the equation would change dramatically should the oil price rise well above $150/barrel. It was this reasoning that prompted President Bush to announce a $720 million funding over five years for the production and distribution of hydrogen for fuel-celled vehicles. Having to import all their oil has forced Japan to be very active in this area, particularly in motor vehicles.

Fuel cell

The fuel cell (FC) works through the reverse of electrolysis, one of the techniques for generating hydrogen and oxygen. Instead of an external source of electrical energy, the FC generates an electric current. The diagram shows the construction of a fuel cell.

Diagram 11. Schematic layout of a fuel cell

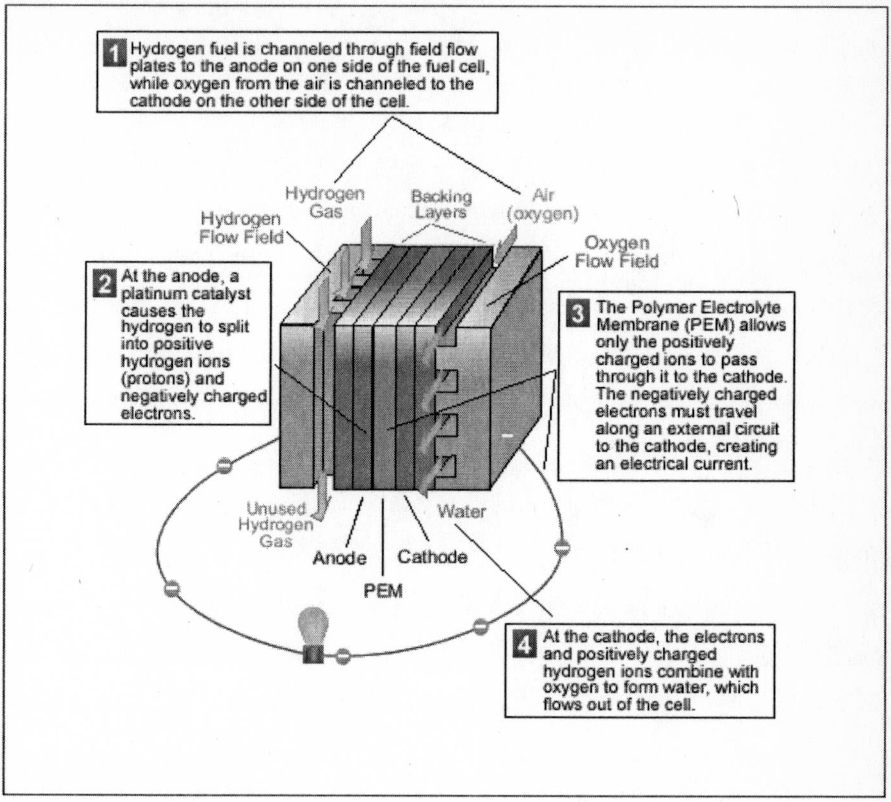

1 Hydrogen fuel is channeled through field flow plates to the anode on one side of the fuel cell, while oxygen from the air is channeled to the cathode on the other side of the cell.

Hydrogen Flow Field

Hydrogen Gas

Backing Layers

Air (oxygen)

Oxygen Flow Field

2 At the anode, a platinum catalyst causes the hydrogen to split into positive hydrogen ions (protons) and negatively charged electrons.

3 The Polymer Electrolyte Membrane (PEM) allows only the positively charged ions to pass through it to the cathode. The negatively charged electrons must travel along an external circuit to the cathode, creating an electrical current.

Unused Hydrogen Gas

Water

Anode   Cathode

PEM

4 At the cathode, the electrons and positively charged hydrogen ions combine with oxygen to form water, which flows out of the cell.

Source: www.fueleconomy.gov

This shows hydrogen entering the anode where a catalyst divides the ions (protons in this case) from the electrons – the former are passed through the electrolyte to the cathode, where they recombine with the electrons that have been round the circuit and react with oxygen to form water. The product is water. Other fuel cells use hydrocarbons instead of hydrogen but the products are the environmentally unfriendly carbon dioxide, sulphur and nitrogen oxides. The process using a polymer electrode is called the Proton Exchange Membrane (PEM).

The PEM construction uses plates either of stainless steel or, more usually, carbon, graphite or reinforced polymer. In most cases the catalyst is in a membrane electrode assembled with the electrolyte between the two plates; when the cell is run at high temperatures, noble metals are used. A typical cell produced 0.6/7 volts, so a stack would be needed to generate 24 or 48 volts. This flexibility is beneficial when running a vehicle at different speeds.

By late 2007, the price of platinum or palladium to make a kilowatt of electricity was expensive at $1,000, but different materials are being tried to reduce the precious metal content. Another problem is the internal resistance of the cell that produces a voltage drop as the current rises which, like an internal combustion engine, can be useful for heating a vehicle. Operating temperatures range from the PEM-type cell at 70 degrees, Celsius up to 1,000 degrees Celsius with a solid oxide construction.

Despite these limitations, the electrical efficiency of a fuel cell itself is usually estimated at around 50% – the best fuels being the basic hydrogen and oxygen configuration. When other losses are taken into consideration, the overall automobile efficiency is about 45% at low loads – around double that claimed for diesel engine cars. A number of applications have been developed taking account of the high reliability of an energy source with no moving parts.

These are some of them:

- Static energy installations with high efficiencies in remote areas such as space crafts are ideal for FCs. One particular closed-circuit programme operating in the state of Washington uses solar panels to produce electricity that in turn electrolyses hydrogen. This is stored at 200psi before passing to the fuel cell (see References). The cells are more efficient if they are combined with the need to generate heat such as in factories, vehicles or homes. At present the capital costs of this type of installation would not yield economic returns.

- The first public hydrogen refuelling station is in Reykjavik, Iceland. It started operation in 2003, serving buses driven by fuel cells with the hydrogen electrolysed by hydropower. Other PEM transports are boats, cars and motorcycles. Boeing and Airbus are experimenting with fuel cells for auxiliary power units (APUs).

Solar power

Solar power has already been mentioned as a means of electrolysing hydrogen as part of an in-line power unit – part of mankind's continuing quest for harnessing the force driving life on earth. Earlier chapters have shown how the sun actuates the food chain. Now solar power is coming into its own as a means of generating electricity or as a source of heat. Previously only useful in the sunbelts, innovations are making solar power viable in temperate zones.

The idea of generating a current from the sun using photovoltaic cells goes back to around the middle of the nineteenth century, but the concept of generating free power has become a priority with the rising cost of fossil fuels, so that by 2007 some 6 megawatts had been installed. One of the reasons slowing development was the high installation cost, which reduced from around $100/watt in the 1970s to $4.50 early in the twenty-first century – the limiting factor being the supply shortage of refined silicon. One important use is to create electrical energy for driving chemical plants such as electrolysis, or for smelting metals using batteries to store energy.

The US was the first country to use solar water heaters commercially in the 1890s, but affordable units only became widely available after the Second World War. By 2006, 104 gigawatts (billion watts) of solar heating was installed globally, with China being a world leader; in Israel 90% of all homes use this technology.

At its simplest, solar heaters employ a grid of pipes backed by a reflector facing the sun at midday through which water is pumped and the hot water stored in an insulated tank. A more sophisticated unit could use brine as the conductor and a form of heat exchanger for domestic use.

The efficiency of thermo-electricity has been improved by using Concentrating Solar Thermal (CST) technology. Here, intense light is focused on heat receivers driven by computer controlled mirrors or lenses that track the sun. This heats fluids to temperatures of up to 1,500 degrees Celsius; at these levels superheated steam can be used to drive turbo generators that supply excess power to the grid by day then draw power at night.

One of the most effective storage mediums is molten salts that are safe and cheaper to use than more sophisticated chemicals. During the heating cycle, saline temperatures between 290 and 565 degrees Celsius can be stored in insulated tanks; these are converted into steam through heat exchangers and turbo generators during the power cycle. Other mediums employ the latent heat of materials that are converted to a liquid or gas in the charging cycle, then returning heat in the power phase. Power is stored in lead/acid combination batteries that can hold current for a few days with high efficiencies; direct current now needs an inverter for conversion to alternating current.

British firm QinetiQ is testing a solar-powered vehicle – Zephyr – an unmanned aerial vehicle (UAV) that weighs only 30 kilograms despite a wingspan of 18 metres. Thin silica compound arrays imbedded in the wings supply current for a propeller and lithium-sulphur batteries for night flying. The opportunities for creating a relatively cheap UAV have obvious attractions for the battlefield and also for civilian security applications.

Great strides are being made to reduce the cost of solar capture and to extend the possibilities for its use outside the sunbelts. One such firm is Flisom AG based in Zurich that plans to market a coated polythene sheet produced in a continuous process. First, the laminar is coated with an absorbent material then cadmium sulphide or zinc selenium is deposited, followed by a final oxide or metalised film. More work needs to be done, but by 2009 it is estimated that the cost of sheeting will be reduced to $1/watt and efficient installations will be made possible even in temperate zones. Another company active in this field is the large American corporation Applied Materials based in California; they are leaders in nanotechnology and specialise in semiconductor chips, flat panel solar displays, solar photovoltaic cells and so on.

References

- Cold fusion – en.wikipedia.org/wiki/Cold_fusion

- Economist briefing on UAV's, November 3rd 2007

- Fuel Cell – en.wikipedia.org/wiki/Fuel-cell

- www.inflo@flisom.ch

- MIT Technology Review

- *Nanofuture*, by J. Storrs Hall (Prometheus Books, 2005)

- Nanotechnology – en.wikipedia.org/wiki/Nanotechnology

- Purdue University – www.physorg.com/news

- Purdue University – www.purdue.edu

- Washington State Stuart Island project – www.siei.org

- The Passarell Process – www.waterdesalination.com

9

Blue Gold

Water is clearly going to be a huge global investment theme. In certain parts of the world it may well become the dominant one. It would be wonderful if we could just tap into this like some giant oil well. In practice, however, even though the basic ingredient falls free from the sky, or can be scooped from the sea, it is very difficult for investors to get involved in a serious way. They may need to collect a series of pennies, rather than expect a big bonanza.

The problem comes on several levels.

In the first place, Harold Markovitz demonstrated that the most profit was derived from the macro strategic investment decision of asset allocation, rather than the micro stock selection one. The broad economic cycle is dominant. Cash or bonds, then equities, then commodity-related positions tended to trend in sequence. Each asset class has to wait its turn for a walk on the sunny side of the street. A recession or housing slump in the USA could have a negative impact on a water-related investment on the other side of the world.

Globalisation increases the power of the butterfly effect.

Problems of true exposure

A company that supplies pipes, valves, and water hydrants in Asia may also be a large supplier to the US housing market. Its share price is more likely to trade on the basis of the latter factors rather than the former.

A company like GE may indeed have a huge international business in desalination equipment, but this activity is dwarfed by the remainder of the business contained in this huge conglomerate. Although included in a portfolio of stocks relevant to water, the share price will perform like a giant of the US stock market. It is a major constituent of – and highly correlated to – the Dow Jones Index.

Just because a company calls itself a water company, or makes a product that relates directly to water, does not mean that as an investment it will perform like a water stock. The whole idea of investing in the growth potential of water is more difficult than just putting together a portfolio of stocks related to the sector. This is the problem that the creators of exchange traded funds have. They have often found it difficult to get their water portfolio to perform well, when the broad stock market indices are in a bear phase.

But for many investors, a fund may still be the best way to incorporate a positive view on water into their portfolios.

Service or commodity

Water is not easy to transport long distances without massive infrastructure. For this reason, in the West water supply companies tend to be local and not national. They lend themselves brilliantly well to being a monopoly. The controls on them tend to be political, and the product behaves like a service rather than a commodity.

The shares of a water utility tend to perform like any other utility. They are not normally seen as glamorous, high growth prospects and they do not achieve such a rating. They are in fact treated as much more like a bond.

Economic cycles are relevant

In a recession water use drops significantly, and water stocks fall along with all the others. Therefore, the overall economic cycles are relevant. We relate to these cycles using the model published by Joseph Schumpeter in the 1930s. This shows that there are long secular trends that can last 20 years or so. Around these are shorter cycles, specifically a 4-year Kitchin wave, and a 10-year Juglar wave. There will be times when these all rise together, creating very profitable opportunities. However, for most of the time, they interact in a complex, non-linear way.

So instead of thinking that, "water is important, let's put some money into it" as if we had discovered a new oil well, we should regard such investments more like plants in a garden. They do not all bloom at the same time, and they need tending and weeding, on a regular basis.

Some basic facts

Use of water is proportional to population, but at a geared rate. The growth in the use of water is roughly double that of population growth. In the poorer countries of the emerging or third world, millions do not have access to clean water. In the rich countries it is used to make a golf course green in a desert.

The total world population is forecast to grow from just over 6 billion to over 9 billion in the next 25 years. Some forecasts have the figure growing to 11 billion by 2050. One can be suspicious of making linear forecasts that far into the future, as it is likely the universe unfolds in cycles. But the exact numbers are not important – the order of magnitude of the problem is.

Diet multiplier

As emerging countries become wealthier there tends to be a change in the diet. This moves slowly but surely from a predominantly vegetarian diet to one including more meat. It takes plenty of water to grow crops to eat, but if the crops are fed to animals first for meat then the need for water increases dramatically. Depending on crop and the animal the multiplier can be anywhere between 100 and 1,000 times.

For example, it takes 600 litres of water to grow the wheat to make a loaf of bread, but 40,000 litres for the equivalent of one kilo of best beef. To grow the crops that would make 1 litre of ethanol takes 12,000 litres of water. This product would take a large SUV about 10 miles at best, or it could supply 300 people with a day's normal use for all domestic purposes.

The cost of affluence

As affluence increases normal domestic use of water goes from being just enough to drink, to, in the West, an absolute minimum of 20 litres per person per day or up to more than 100 times that. It is used freely for not just drinking and cooking, but washing and cleaning the car, all the way up to the all important green golf course in a desert.

The tropics are growing

The greatest stress on the planet's ability to provide this water is greater in the tropics than anywhere else. However, if the forecasts of Raymond Wheeler and others are correct about the likely changes in the climate then the tropics are going to extend by about 300 more miles north and south. This change will put millions – who currently do not have a water problem – into a position where they will need to budget more carefully.

It's in the price

Modern markets are supposed to be very efficient at allocating resources. However, in the case of water it is almost impossible to have a fair pricing system that would work on a global basis, or even a national one. Nature does not put water where humans think they need it most. We experience floods where we do not want water, and droughts where we do. In some parts of Africa, a villager may have to pay the equivalent of £4 to get a plastic jug filled with water that may not be germ free. The contrast with the rich world and its golf course is very marked.

Infrastructure opportunities

In the developed world, water is supplied as a service. It needs to be captured into a reservoir, piped, pumped, stored and delivered for domestic, industrial and agricultural purposes. In the domestic area a third of all the water delivered is flushed down the drain. It needs to be taken away and processed. It is likely to be used again, probably many times over.

All of this needs infrastructure and offers investment opportunities. This includes items as small as washing machines that are more economical on water use than older designs, better showers and smaller baths.

It should not be assumed that because the Western developed world already has such infrastructure that there are no investment opportunities here. On the contrary, many of the pipes and plants were put in during Victorian times or earlier. There is massive replacement demand, and with risk to reward ratios being as they are, these needs will almost certainly take precedence over the developing world.

The World Water Council estimates that about US$80 billion are currently being spent annually in both developed and developing countries. It also believes that more than double this amount will be required continually over the next 20 years.

Industry

In industry, water uses are huge but the structure needs to be different. Water cools nuclear reactors, and other power plants, and in chemical plants it is a large input. Different types of pipes and mechanisms are needed.

Agriculture

Agricultural use in the developed world tends to be efficient. Australia has gone through a seven-year drought which has made them very effective at using every drop well. Their ideas may now be exported to the less developed part of the world. Israel has also developed brilliant irrigation systems that do not waste water to evaporation. These too could be used elsewhere. In underdeveloped countries – even where they have water – the system for irrigation is so simple and basic that only a fraction of the water pumped actually reaches the plants that need it. The vast majority is evaporated back into the atmosphere.

The system developed in Israel, effectively takes the water to the plant in a small diameter pipe, and then releases the water in droplets. This is provided at about the rate that the plant can absorb the water. Almost none goes to waste. The old-fashioned alternative is to pump water from a well and lead it through an open ditch, where it causes a temporary flood to the plants. The relevant countries are almost all, by definition, very hot and dry, so evaporation takes place. If the new system was installed, many of these countries would be able to feed themselves, without needing more water, but just making better use of what they have.

Dust bowl

The USA and Canada have been the bread baskets of a fair proportion of the world, but the forecasts from the Raymond Wheeler cycles make it more likely that these areas will come under stress. One of his dominant cycles is approximately 100 years long, and does seem to fit with the longer economic cycle.

Just at the time when many shrewd investors like George Soros are saying that we are going to have the worst economic experience since the 1930s, so are the weather forecasts looking to potentially dust bowl conditions. Even if the degree of the problem is not as extreme this time the direction clearly points to a need for water conservation.

Technology

Desalination of salt water is already a big business and will in future inevitably grow larger. After all, this planet is not short of water, it could even be thought of as having a gross excess off it. The problem is that it is not in a form that humans can use it. Taking water from the sea requires energy. Doing this on a vast scale is possible for countries that have an ample supply of cheap energy, as in the Middle East. However, this method is not going to work on a global scale.

An ideal marriage is possible with solar power, or possibly wind power. The very countries most stressed by the water condition are in the tropics, and automatically blessed with too much sunshine. Large fields of solar cells linked to desalination equipment could turn a desert into a green and pleasant land. If political issues can be overcome the technology exists to produce a very beneficial outcome. The developed world has the technology and the money, and the emerging world has the land, the sun, and the sea in abundance. It should not be beyond the wit of man to put these ingredients together.

Hydrogen

The coupling above could get even better.

All over the world, manufacturers are preparing for the end to total reliance on oil. Even if peak oil is well in the future, relative to our lives, the concept is still valid that other sources will need to be developed.

One fuel with a good future is hydrogen. It can already work in existing internal combustion engines. Motor car makers like this. The only limit is whether the public can buy hydrogen to fill up their vehicles. States like California are possibly setting the lead in providing the infrastructure for this to take place. Even if the internal combustion engine reaches the end of its growth, hydrogen can still continue to grow as it works fuel cells. It is not the only fuel to do so, but it is the cleanest. The side product is not toxic exhaust, but water.

This is the vision for a great investment.

A country with a lot of low cost land near the sea: this can have huge solar cell plants covering many acres. Using the sun's energy they desalinate the sea. Some of this water can turn the land green and service a luxury domestic lifestyle. Some of the water can be diverted to a hydrogen making plant also using the suns power. This can then be used in vehicles, power stations, and fuel cells. If the right investments were made this would turn some currently valueless desert into priceless real estate.

Keep it clean

Another huge industry related to water involves keeping it clean. Many diseases are carried by water. Especially in the poorest countries it is the life-giving water that often causes most deaths. Rather than spend money on medicine after the disease has spread, it would be more cost-effective to keep the water clean. There will be growth opportunities for chemical, and drug companies, as well as bio-tech ones. As this is a big problem, the solution should give rise to big investment opportunities.

It is not only the developing nations that have this problem. Lake Ontario is one of the largest bodies of fresh water on the planet and yet over 100 impurities have been identified within it. This water has to contain chlorine and be treated before it can be drinkable, and even those who simply swim in it find that it can cause severe skin irritation.

Summary

The ways to invest in water can be listed as follows:

- Own **water rights**. These tend to be local monopolies. There may be a tendency for a large parent company to buy up many such rights to make a national, or at least regional, player, but there is little logic to this. However, there are some vast reservoirs and lakes that cover a huge geographical area. There are a few global operators in this activity like Veolia Environment.

- Companies that provide **infrastructure products** from pipes to pumps. These are equally important, both for initial supply and for the removal and treatment of waste. Also, desalination equipment and the membranes and chemicals used to process water to keep it clean.

- **Exchange traded funds**, which may be the best answer for many investors.

Afterword

History does not repeat itself, it rhymes
Mark Twain

The further back you look, the further forward you can see
Winston Churchill

We have embarked on a voyage, even a pilgrimage, on the role water plays in our lives and how it will shape the future. In the previous chapters we looked backwards to the Green Revolution that allowed millions to prosper, and forwards to the frightening legacy of those who have abused it or taken it for granted.

However, much of what we have written about is on few people's mainstream agenda and needs to be integrated with such matters as potential bank failures, the global credit crunch, religious terrorism, even man-made global warming. For this reason we have decided that this Afterword should not only pull together our work on water, but also incorporate it with the current strands of economic, political and business thinking to consider the much wider implications. For example, how is the individual to adjust to the possibility of rising food prices at the same time as a recession that will put him out of work; or how should a company orientate itself to future business? Probably most important, **have governments in the developed world the resources or the people to deal with a potential crisis on a scale not seen for decades – even centuries?**

In the early decades of the twenty-first century, there are three destabilising dynamics:

1. **water** is clearly a major one,

2. another is the threat of **religious terrorism**, and

3. the third is the bursting of the **credit bubble** in the form of a growing credit crunch in the Western world.

We can examine each of these in more detail in an attempt to generate scenarios and to identify leading indicators.

1. Water

Water-related problems such as conflicts are dependent on the climatic shifts, increasing desertification and volcanic eruptions explained in earlier chapters. These then make their incidence a good basis for judging the severity of any refugee problems, food shortages, the potential for revolutions or conflicts. We can now divide these into three levels of severity.

Level One

The Pacific La Nina proves to be slight, and in the Atlantic flooding in northern Europe due to mild volcanic eruptions in Russia are tolerable. In this context China, Pakistan and North Korea can back-up any food shortfalls with imports from North or South America, and in the Middle East an uneasy truce continues, although progress is made harnessing Israeli food technology to the region.

Level Two

Oscillations become more pronounced, volcanic eruptions are more severe and sunspots remain low, which only accentuate the impact of the La Nina on both sides of the Pacific. This impacts on food production in the sensitive Asian and Middle East areas that can only marginally be made up by imports from the Americas, that are themselves facing shortages; food rockets in price followed by other commodities and there are concerns in the West about continuity of supply.

The refugee problems accelerate: moving from Central Asia into Eastern Europe and east to China. The flow from Africa accelerates into a water-starved southern Europe, and out of China to Indonesia and into Australia. At the same time, preparations are made to deal with epidemics caused by the newcomers. Military manoeuvres are observed in the countries most affected, so prompting talks of re-armament in the West, India and Japan.

Level Three

Level Three embraces the worst possible condition where the ocean oscillations force the rain belts away from high areas of population and major volcanic activity reduces global temperature by up to 3 degrees Fahrenheit on average – this could be doubled if sunspots remain at another minimum. There is starvation in northern China, Central Asia, parts of the Middle East and elsewhere, that forces desperate people to move. The extreme cold forces restrictions on oil and gas supplies from Canada and Russia, resulting in massive rises in the cost of energy. There is radical action to accelerate the development of alternative fuels such as hydrogen.

Co-ordinated military action by Iran, Pakistan, China and North Korea obliges the West to urgently implement re-armament plans in support of India and to keep open the Gulf oilfields. Western governments, squeezed by reduced revenues and with military and refugee commitments, are forced to reduce spending on the welfare state with consequential privatisation (see below). At the same time they will probably be obliged to deal with rocketing food prices causing major unrest in affected countries and the prospects of pandemics and breakaway national divisions.

2. Religious terrorism

Religious terrorism is a growing threat to the developed world largely generated by :Wahabism, a strict Sunni Islamic sect funded by oil money; another is the growing possibility of Iran developing nuclear weapons; and finally the ability of Al-Qaeda to challenge the West economically through rising oil prices, hacking into vital networks or attempting to destroy its currency. Again, these can be developed into three levels.

Level One

Level One confines action to the occasional terrorist act similar to Baader-Meinhoff, ETA or the IRA. The present interchange of information continues and the security forces manage to thwart most potential outrages. The oil price below $110/barrel and attempts at hacking are thwarted.

Level Two

Level Two sees an accelerating influence of the militant Wahabis, which prompts much greater vigilance; increased resources to homeland security in the West are needed to counter a rising level of outrage. Tension in the Middle East reaches a new level when the US or Israel attack the Iran nuclear weapons programme with the support of many Sunni-led countries. There are mounting efforts by Iran to close the Strait of Hormuz to allied shipping and the oil price rises to around £180/barrel. The West is obliged to take more draconian measures to protect their homeland.

Level Three

Level Three could trigger the great battle of Armageddon forecast in the Revelations to St. John where the demonic forces are defeated by God's armies. The site of Megiddo, just by the Plain of Jezreel, has seen many conflicts over the ages and it is possible that this ends militancy. Another outrage could be an atomic blast in a major Western city that forces an all-out attack on terrorist forces.

3. Credit crunch

The term *credit crunch* has been used extensively after the first sub-prime failures in the third quarter of 2007. While these have cast shadows over the banking system, the ultimate in a credit crunch is when bad debts become so overwhelming and the pool of available liquidity becomes so small that interest rates are driven up by desperation to a level reflecting the risk and shortages. The credit system then implodes. Again we can identify three levels:

Level One

Level One suggests that the crisis in the banking system can be contained despite the failure of some funds, mortgage lenders and brokers. Although the quantum of total risks remain uncertain, the vigilance of the central banks ensures that there is sufficient liquidity for inter-bank lending and to customers with the highest credit ratings. The US dollar continues to decline against other currencies causing EU and Eastern economies to slow down.

Level Two

The excess liquidity central banks have injected into their economies to contain deflation and to float off debt, shows in rising inflation. This is accentuated by Level Two water problems that fuel rising prices by the cost-push of commodity prices. This unhappy combination can lead either to rising inflation or the much more dangerous condition of stagflation encountered in the early 1970s. Both cause currencies to fall, although stock markets may continue to rise initially.

This propels the central banks into a dilemma: whether to quell the forces of inflation by raising interest rates and risk a recession, or attempt to control inflation by legislation on prices and income that was tried and signally failed three decades earlier. Ultimately, inflation becomes so damaging to communities and nations that interest rates are applied.

Level Three

Level Three is the ultimate nightmare of politicians and bankers as deflation takes hold and all the debt and clever financial instruments that fuelled the previous speculative binge, now implode with the resulting depression, probably on the scale of the 1930s or worse. As government revenues fall they are faced with the prospect of reducing expenditure or destroying the private sector, the only group capable of working the economy out of a recession. Their dilemma may be only partly solved, as it was in the late 1930s, by the prospect of re-armament.

How then are we to think about the dynamics, for the threats from them are very real. Also, do they provide sufficient warning in themselves for anticipatory action to be taken? Although these have been set down at distinct levels, the transition from one to the next may be blurred. For example, the climatic shifts that control water are driven by long-term oscillations whose effect can be seen year by year; however, a major eruption would cause a rapid shift in level. For religious terrorism, the trigger points are likely to be more clear – defined as these are by outrages. The credit crunch levels again may not be immediately defined despite being driven by the most closely watched indicators – although there is an inevitability of a continuing credit vortex. However the levels may be measured, it is essential they be considered as a whole and fall neatly into nine combinations of scenarios.

Even defining the scenarios may not be satisfactory because of the transition problems mentioned earlier so, as in wartime, we are obliged to consider the worst case position and to draw out contingency plans for this possible outcome even though some pressures are immediate. We propose to do this by taking material from the chapters in this book and from *Future Storm* – we can then accommodate any lesser contingency. We will be setting outlines of likely contingency plans for the:

1.   individual,

2.   corporations and

3.   governments.

Individuals

The individual is probably both the greatest loser and the most important survivor. Those who rely on state payments will find much of the life support they have been used to receiving to be greatly changed to one of self-help and the making of individual choices. While it is true that the state cannot withdraw all services from those who rely on them, ways need to be found for providing these without the costs of state overhead. Most important, there needs to be some means of gainfully employing those without work (see below).

On the other hand, those who wish to stand on their own feet should find a propitious environment of low taxes, minimal interest rates and much reduced regulation should governments behave wisely.

Industry and commerce

Industry and commerce will need to adapt to the new environment in at least five ways:

1. Potential markets will, in part, be determined by the climatic cycles. For example, markets or subsidiaries in northern China and other areas affected by drought will become very unstable but could be prime customers for armaments, food and desalination plants.

2. Prime product areas are likely to be energy, mining and food, in addition to products and services associated with water.

3. It is likely that politicians will attempt to raise tariff barriers so restricting commercial activity to new trading blocs.

4. The present structure of corporations will need to be refashioned to make them much more adaptable to rapidly changing conditions. Part of the transformation will oblige organisations to reduce overheads and fixed costs, and to devise new management structures.

5. It is possible that the present financial globalised structures will implode and return to much more localised banking and fund-raising.

State

The state will be obliged to focus on areas that are currently probably not on politicians' radar screens, although everything in this book is in the public domain. Unlike man-made global warming that is of passing concern, the following Action

Agenda Items (AAI) are most likely to intrude themselves on national programmes within the years to 2020 – some being very immediate. Ten essential policy items for action are proposed:

1. Improving the use of water and reclaiming arable land

Improving the use of water and reclaiming arable land (some third of the 1.5 billion hectares currently available) must become a major international issue unless many are to perish. Chapters 2 and 3 showed the present gross waste of transferring and using water and allowing the destruction of arable land in many parts of the world, but rising desertification (shown in Diagram 12) can only increase the problem. For example, new methods of farming in Europe will require different husbandry, while people tilling the freshly watered land are unlikely to have either adequate equipment or the will for large-scale farming.

Item 6 proposes that a civilian army be mobilised and trained to introduce modern methods such as those employed in Israel. These will come from the unemployed in developed countries and the many available in developing countries that have seen a rising population; Item 6 suggests how these may be recruited and trained to perform national and international tasks.

Diagram 12: The impact of increased desertification on southern Europe

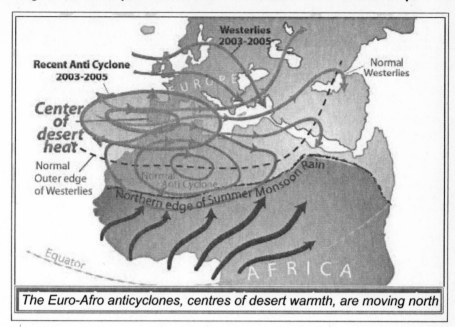

The Euro-Afro anticyclones, centres of desert warmth, are moving north

Source: Browning Newsletter

2. Making provision for refugees

Making provision for refugees on the lines described in Chapter 5. Domestically there will be additional threats to the West from associated diseases.

3. Middle East settlement

A Middle East settlement rests in large part by exchanging peace for water competence. The major players in any peace accord are likely to be Turkey and Israel (described in Chapter 6).

4. Conflict in Asia

Conflict in Asia would be triggered should the water threat move to Level 2 and drought stirs internal conflict in China; if this were accompanied by a loss of face associated with a failure of the Olympics, the pressure of the authorities to act

would be almost overwhelming. The major contenders in the axis are likely to be China, Iran, Pakistan and North. Korea. With the prime target for China being Burma, with its energy, water, food and mineral resources, the first priority for the West must be to secure oil supplies (by preventing attempts to block the Strait of Hormuz) and to support India. This could extend to a more general re-armament (as set out in Chapter 7).

5. Homeland Security

Homeland Security will become an increasing threat should terrorism move to Level 2. This, or a move to Level 3, would oblige politicians to consider wartime measurers such as internment, forfeit of citizenship, abrogation of human and Habeas Corpus rights. The action should extend to disease control and measures to limit disruption to essential services through computer hacking.

6. Creation of a civilian army

The creation of a civilian army to work at home and abroad. Raised from the unemployed and with an embedded training curriculum, they would perform national and international relief such as the restoration programmes AAI 1 and 2 described earlier. This is an organisation based on the Civilian Conservation Corps (CCC) initiated by President Roosevelt in 1933. It took young men from deprived homes, trained them in practical outdoor work and in aspects of disaster relief.

The new concept, let us call it the Conservation and Security Administration (CSA), takes the CCC principle a stage further by suggesting a wider and vital international role that could be largely managed by existing private organisations in English-speaking countries. As in the 1930s, this would have the effect of considerably reducing crime and, at the same time, diminishing such life-debilitating habits as obesity and idleness; so providing individuals with skills and pride of purpose and achievement.

7. Create an environment in which individuals can thrive

Create an environment for individuals to thrive on the proven principle that people bring a country out of recession, not governments. These arrangements to include low taxation and interest rates, minimum regulation and a propitious environment to succeed; regulations imposed by states and unions will be voided. As many people are likely to want independence, there will be a growing demand for tried business formats such as those provided by franchising.

8. Manage asset deflation and secure the clearing banking system

In August 2007, the world felt the first stages of a debt deflation that has the capacity to swamp the traditional safeguards. The security of the commercial banks is fundamental to the economic survival in any society, as the Japanese discovered in the 1990s when rising bad debts helped to abort any recovery. The same problem could be with us again, the first being the very amateurish attempt to rescue Northern Rock, a British mortgage bank.

Central bankers will have to managing the huge quantity of debt that will require a fine balance between injecting liquidity, government support guarantees, reducing taxes and interest rates. For protecting the commercial banks we should return to a position similar to 1933, after 4,004 banks failed in the US with a depositor loss of around $4 billion, although most received up to 85% in compensation later.

The solution was the Glass-Steagall Act of 1933 that created the Federal Deposit Insurance Corporation (FDIC) as a regulatory body to monitor and, if necessary, force a bank into insolvency. Funded by insurance payments levied on the vast majority of US banks, the FDIC has five categories of risk.

The first are the well capitalised banks with capital ratios of 10% to liquid assets or higher, the second level are concerns with a ratio of 8% or better; these are classed as adequately capitalised. Undercapitalised banks, at less than 8%, are given a remedial warning, and if the ratio falls below 6%, the FDIC has the authority to remove the management and force corrective action. If the ratio falls below 2% the

FDIC declares the bank insolvent, deposits of at least $100,000 are transferred to a solvent bank, the bad debts are sterilised and the good loans sold on.

This system worked well even in the case of the Continental and Illinois failure in 1984, although the Savings and Loans crisis in the 1980s required $150 billion in federal funds. Now the FDIC has funds of $49 billion, but this may be quite inadequate when the mortgage collapse alone could cost upwards of $500 billion. This does not take into account many investment banks that have become involved in securitising assets and in credit derivatives that could become a systemic threat to security.

9. Encourage new technology

Encourage new technology (such as those proposed in Chapter 8) to make developed countries less dependent upon imported energy. In particular, encourage the use of hydrogen as an alternative fuel and solar heating as a source of localised energy. In addition, there is the need to develop new water-saving crops and the possibility of producing synthetic food.

10. Prepare to downsize governments

Prepare to reduce governments should any of the threats move to Level 2. Since the Second World War, the state has taken on increasing responsibilities to provide welfare support on the principle that these can be afforded and managed with rising growth. This assumption can no longer be taken for granted and ways must be found to privatise public services such as health, education and welfare that the state often performs only indifferently, and increase spending on the other areas vital to security.

History also helps determine what the state should not do:

- **Do not institute large-scale public work programmes**

  These were tried in the US during the 1930s and in Japan in the 1990s. Both failed to revive their respective economies and only succeeded in increasing national debt and ballooning budget deficits.

- **Do not erect tariff barriers, they only attract retaliation**

  One of the greatest errors of the US in 1930 was to pass the Smoot-Hawley Act that raised tariffs on a wide range of agricultural products during a secular decline in commodity prices. Other countries retaliated, which hastened a rapid decline in world trade.

- **Do not attempt to float away debt by causing hyperinflation**

  It was one of the causes that destroyed the Roman Empire; while in France the *assignat* became worthless and paved the way for Napoleonic tyranny. Lenin used it to bankrupt the bourgeoisie, and in Germany the printing presses in 1923/4 helped to herald the rise of Hitler's Nazis.

Stages of required action

We can now consider several stages of implementing the ten actions based on the state of affairs in early 2008.

Stage 1

Even when each of the dynamics are at benign levels there is a clear need for all nations to initiate a programme to help arrest the major degradation of arable land. Even if initiatives are taken early in 2008, it would take a year for any programme to be mobilised, when even more land would have been taken out of production. At this stage of the credit cycle, it is essential for each nation without an FDIC-type programme to initiate action. It would also be essential for other nations to follow the lead of the US to develop hydrogen as an alternative fuel.

Stage 2

Stage 2 could easily occur during the latter quarter of 2008 or 2009, when the climatic shifts and credit cycle could deteriorate. Then it would be essential to make contingency plans to manage refugees and to make urgent plans to mobilise a Middle East settlement to avoid a more devastating conflict later. At this point a very close watch needs to be kept on China, Iran, Pakistan and North Korea for signs of potential mobilisation and troop movements that would require a response from the allies. This is the period when a major volcanic action can be expected that would move the climatic shifts quickly to Level 3; this would make food production a premium at the expense of any ethanol programme and accelerate moves to…

Stage 3

This is the full mobilisation of all items on the Action Agenda, except possibly homeland security, although there would be the expectation that terrorists would try to strike nations already reeling from high food and energy prices. Unwinding the welfare state will probably be the most difficult for politicians to conceive or implement.

State competence probably reached its peak during the Second World War, when it was able to attract the most able individuals to manage the departments of state during the emergency. More recently, fewer experienced individuals have entered politics and those that have tend to be professional politicians unable to cope with the management of large departments; a coalition would be needed, as in wartime, to attract the best people.

In addition, many of the AAI programmes will need an international perspective and ability such as those provided by the Allies planning and executing the Overlord invasion of Europe. The major players, once again, are likely to be the English-speaking peoples acting in concert with like-minded countries, but other groups may emerge such as the Carolingian Group of France and Germany in association with

Russia. Ideally, implementing these plans should be the remit of the United Nations – but it is unlikely that much of this organisation will survive a major crisis.

This all sounds very gloomy, but our forefathers have been here before. Out of the Dark Ages emerged the prosperity and glorious cathedrals of the thirteenth century. The horrors of the Black Death of the fourteenth century gave way to freeing the serfs in England and the Italian Renaissance. Three centuries later, the Enlightenment developed from the chaos of the seventeenth century. Now, we believe, a new golden age will emerge from the difficulties that lie ahead.

In each case it was able individuals, not kings, presidents or dictators, who saw the new opportunities presented by a warmer climate, a powerful vision or a united country and led the way to new prosperity. But what is the calibre of the individuals now aspiring to lead us?

- Can it be the **central bankers**, terrified of deflations, who allowed interest rates to remain low for so long that it encouraged an orgy of financial and housing speculation?

- Could it be the **financial engineers**, who created packages priced by clever formulas that elevated sub-prime mortgages into premium products, then selling them to gullible investors leaving others to clean up the mess?

- Perhaps it will be **politicians**, who encouraged over-indebted individuals to continue spending to substantiate their claim to have created economic miracles?

- Maybe it will be the hubris of **other politicians**, locked the time warp of their student days who, despite all the historical evidence, preach the primacy of the state's ability to run complex organisations or solve every problem?

We are convinced that, as in the past, individuals will arise in countries where there is a tradition of politicians who believe they are the people's servants – what James Bennett calls the *Anglosphere Challenge* (see References). This provides hope, but how could they emerge? There are probably two conditions:

1. there is a belief that the old order has failed, and

2. there has to be a crisis.

Michael Lewitt, the editor of HCM (see References), identifies what scientists call *path dependency* as the continuing cause of failed policies. This describes a phenomenon whereby once a technological standard is adopted, the benefit of using it increases and it becomes more expensive to shift to another technology. Lewitt applies this to the methodology for selling sub-prime mortgages, but it applies to many different walks of life. The way to disrupt the path is to show the earlier principle no longer works, but this requires a crisis – as the sub-prime debacle did so spectacularly.

Co-author Robin Griffiths describes what is known in investment circles as the four steps to disillusion:

1. The first step in any set-back in a stock price is to **disregard it**. 'It is nothing to worry about.'

2. The second is to **fight the new trend** by pouring in more assets.

3. The third is **capitulation** – 'I'm out'.

4. The fourth is to ask '**what do I do now?**'

Referring to the risks described previously, the path of dependency will probably not be shaken by Level 1 – equivalent to the First Step of disillusion. Even Level 2 of the credit bubble might not shake the path, although the onset of Level 2 water might do this, as it would be largely unexpected – bread riots would shake the confidence of any politician. At some point the Fourth Step question will be raised, the signal for a latter-day Winston Churchill to emerge, who has already prepared us for a new path and will lead us along it.

We can only speculate where the path may lead. Will it be the Third Wave described in Alvin Toffler's eponymous book, where the individual at last becomes dominant? Another, might be a decision to return states to a latter-day gold standard where currency decisions are left to the market and we start to rebuild a new industry and society. Whatever happens we can be sure that water will play an important part despite other factors moving onto a broader platform. This book has identified how this molecule will be the driving force, among others, to weave an outcome from a series of problems and will exercise the talents of the most able individuals. Their efforts will be worth it. Emerging from the chaos will be a new golden era in the early decades of the Third Millennium after Christ.

References

- *Anglosphere Challenge, The*, by James C. Bennett (Rowman & Littlefield, 2007)

- *HCM Market Letter, The*, by Michael Lewitt (www.hegcap.com)

Index

U

Uganda 70

Ukraine 20

unemployment 99

United Nations High Commissioner for Refugees (UNHCR) 65

United States, the xiv, 5-7, 79, 90, 119

V

Vietnam 108, 117

volcanic activity 1-2, 24, 38, 61

    economic impact of 15-16

volcanoes 14

W

Wallace, Henry 42

warm/dry areas 62

warm/dry phase 60

warm/wet places 61

warm/wet phase 59

water

    conflict over 105

    consumption 37, 41, 86

    controlling 24, 136

    distributing 27

    financial implications 55

    husbanding 27

    hybrids that can use substandard water 42

    investing in 133

    molecular structure 19

    potential deficit areas 38

    preserving 24

    recirculation of 30

    regenerating 28

    retention 41

    states it can exist in 19

    supply of 55, 139

    surplus countries 115

    treatment plants 29-30

    use of 24, 31, 41, 86

water-borne diseases 28, 30, 75

waste water 28-29

West Coast 5

wheat 43, 110-111

wheel line irrigation 28

Wheeler, Professor Raymond xv, 49, 51, 53, 56, 58, 61, 136

White Nile 9

wind 22

Wolf Minimum 3

World Bank 89

World Water Council 137

Y

Yangtze river 108, 112

Yellow River, see 'Hwang Ho'